Northern Ireland since 1968

Making Contemporary Britain Series

General Editor: Anthony Seldon
Consultant Editor: Peter Hennessy

Published

Northern Ireland since 1968
Paul Arthur and Keith Jeffery

The Prime Minister since 1945
James Barber

British General Elections since 1945
David Butler

The British Economy since 1945
Alec Cairncross

Britain and the Suez Crisis
David Carlton

The End of the British Empire
John Darwin

Religion in Britain since 1945
Grace Davie

British Defence since 1945
Michael Dockrill

British Politics since 1945
Peter Dorey

Britain and the Falklands War*
Lawrence Freedman

Britain and European Integration
since 1945
Stephen George

British Social Policy since 1945
Howard Glennerster

Judicial Politics since 1920:
A Chronicle
John Griffith

Consensus Politics from Attlee to
Major
Dennis Kavanagh and Peter Morris

The Politics of Immigration
Zig Layton-Henry

Women in Britain since 1945
Jane Lewis

Britain and the Korean War*
Callum Macdonald

Culture in Britain since 1945
Arthur Marwick

Crime and Criminal Justice since 1945
Terence Morris

The British Press and Broadcasting
since 1945
Colin Seymour-Ure

Third Party Politics since 1945
John Stevenson

The Labour Party since 1945
Eric Shaw

The Trade Union Question in British
Politics
Robert Taylor

The Civil Service since 1945
Kevin Theakston

British Science and Politics since
1945
Thomas Wilkie

British Public Opinion
Robert M. Worcester

Forthcoming

British Industry since 1945
Margaret Ackrill

British Foreign Policy since 1945
Anthony Adamthwaite

The Conservative Party since 1945
John Barnes

Town Planning in Britain since 1900
Gordon Cherry

Electoral Change since 1945
Pippa Norris

Sport in Britain since 1945
Richard Holt and Tony Mason

Class and Inequality in Britain since 1945
Paul Keating

Parliament since 1945
Philip Norton

British Youth Cultures since 1945
William Osgerby

Terrorism since 1945
Paul Wilkinson

Local Government since 1945
Ken Young and Nirmala Rao

* Indicates title now out of print.

The series *Making Contemporary Britain* is essential reading for students, as well as providing masterly overviews for the general reader. Each book in the series puts the central themes and problems of the specific topic into clear focus. The studies are written by leading authorities in their field, who integrate the latest research into the text but at the same time present the material in a clear, ordered fashion which can be read with value by those with no prior knowledge of the subject.

THE INSTITUTE OF CONTEMPORARY
BRITISH HISTORY

Senate House
Malet Street
London WC1H 7HU

First published 1988
Reprinted 1989 (twice)
Second edition 1996

Blackwell Publishers Ltd
108 Cowley Road
Oxford OX4 1JF

Blackwell Publishers Inc.
238 Main Street
Cambridge, Massachusetts 02142
USA

British Library Cataloguing in Publication Data
A CIP catalogue record for this book is available from the British Library.
Library of Congress Cataloging-in-Publication Data
Arthur, Paul, 1945–
   Northern Ireland since 1968 / Paul Arthur and Keith Jeffery. — 2nd ed.
      p.   cm. — (Making contemporary Britain)
   Includes bibliographical references and index.
   ISBN 0–631–20084–3 (pbk.)
      1. Northern Ireland—History—1969–1994.   I. Jeffery, Keith.
   II. Title.   III. Series.
   DA990.U46A75   1996   95–41639
   941.60824—dc20   CIP

This book is printed on acid-free paper

Contents

General Editor's Preface   viii

Preface to Second Edition   x

List of Abbreviations   xiii

1 Introduction   1
2 The Northern Ireland Political Landscape   5
3 A Place Apart   21
4 Unionist Politics   34
5 Nationalist Politics   53
6 Keeping the Peace   66
7 The International Dimension   82
8 Politics as Process   99
9 Conclusion   124

Appendix: Deaths Caused by the Violence in
Northern Ireland, 1969–1994   129

Outline Chronology   130

Dramatis Personae   135

Further Reading   138

Index   139

General Editor's Preface

The Institute of Contemporary British History's series *Making Contemporary Britain* is aimed directly at students and at others interested in learning more about topics in post-war British history. In the series, authors are less attempting to break new ground than presenting clear and balanced overviews of the state of knowledge on each of the topics.

The ICBH was founded in October 1986 with the objective of promoting the study of British history since 1945 at every level. To that end, it publishes books and a quarterly journal, *Contemporary Record*; it organizes seminars and conferences for school students, undergraduates, researchers and teachers of post-war history; and it runs a number of research programmes and other activities.

A central theme of the ICBH's work is that post-war history is too often neglected in British schools, institutes of higher education and beyond. The ICBH acknowledges the validity of the arguments against the study of recent history, notably the problems of bias, of overly subjective teaching and writing and the difficulties of perspective. But it believes that the values of studying post-war history outweigh the drawbacks, and that the health and future of a liberal democracy require that its citizens know more about the most recent past of their country than the limited knowledge possessed by British citizens, young and old, today. Indeed, the ICBH believes that the dangers of political indoctrination are higher where the young are *not* informed of the recent past.

The second edition of this popular book is most welcome, and long overdue. Much has changed in Ireland in the eight years since the first edition of *Northern Ireland since 1968* first appeared, not least the cease-fire and a change in the terms of dialogue between the parties to the peace process.

The authors have resisted the temptation merely to bolt on a few updated paragraphs to their former text. Instead, the book has been extensively rewritten, and an entirely new chapter ('Politics as Process') has been added. Readers will be delighted at the commitment that the authors have given to the task: the second edition retains all the strengths that made the first edition one of the most valued and popular texts on Northern Ireland, but they have also made it in many ways into a work that deserves to be regarded as an entirely new book.

Anthony Seldon

living in a different political climate globally and parochially. The starkest example of the latter lies in the peace process which has the potential to remove us once and for all from an intimidatory political culture. We are conscious of the emergence of a new political vocabulary where concepts such as 'process' and 'inclusivity' are coming into play. This edition needs to reflect these changes in psyche and political activity. Obviously we have added greater detail to each chapter. But we implore the reader to be conscious of the nuances created in a different political climate.

We thank reviewers of the first edition for their comments and have attempted to incorporate any positive criticism into the narrative.

Abbreviations

CDU	Campaign for Democracy in Ulster
DUP	Democratic Unionist Party
IIP	Irish Independence Party
INLA	Irish National Liberation Army
IRA	Irish Republican Army
IRSP	Irish Republican Socialist Party
NICRA	Northern Ireland Civil Rights Association
NILP	Northern Ireland Labour Party
NUPRG	New Ulster Political Research Group
PD	People's Democracy
PIRA	Provisional Irish Republican Army
PSF	Provisional Sinn Fein
PUP	Progressive Unionist Party
RIR	Royal Irish Regiment
RUC	Royal Ulster Constabulary
SDLP	Social Democratic and Labour Party
UDA	Ulster Defence Association
UDP	Ulster Democratic Party
UDR	Ulster Defence Regiment
UPRG	Ulster Political Research Group
USCA	Ulster Special Constabulary Association
UUP	Ulster Unionist Party
UUUC	United Ulster Unionist Council
UVF	Ulster Volunteer Force
UWC	Ulster Workers' Council
VPP	Volunteer Political Party
VUP	Vanguard Unionist Party

1 Introduction

One of the clichés concerning the Northern Ireland problem contends that if all the publications, the explanations, the analyses and the solutions to the problem were put side by side they would span the circumference of the world. The problem still remains obscure to many and we believe there is room for this examination of 'the Troubles'.

In the first place, while output may be massive, market research on readership may not be so sophisticated. Even after twenty-five years of violent conflict Northern Ireland rates sparse mention in general VIth form or undergraduate textbooks concerned with contemporary British history and politics. It is as if authors consider it alien to the British political experience. This is rather curious if only because the problem has had a debilitating effect on the political process. One thinks of the obvious, such as the huge security operations which attend every party conference in the aftermath of the attempt to assassinate the prime minister and most of her cabinet at Brighton in 1984. One could add the financial drain which Northern Ireland continues to impose on the Exchequer, the introduction of Draconian legislation which casts doubt on the quality of British democracy and the embarrassment within the international community attached to the conduct of Northern Irish business. Others could be added. In short, Northern Ireland continues to be a major problem on the political agenda, and yet there still seems to be a lack of knowledge in Britain about the conflict.

Secondly, we should heed E. H. Carr's remark that the date of publication can be more revealing than the name of the author on the title page. This first edition of this book was acutely conscious of the significance of the Anglo-Irish Agreement of 1985 which we believe helped to change the nature of the debate within Northern Ireland and the power relationships as a result. The unionist community felt a sense of great betrayal on the part of the sovereign power. Given the unionists' seemingly absolute dominance from 1921 to 1972, and their relative confidence that they could count on an acceptable minimal support in Great Britain, particularly from a Conservative government, it is difficult to convey the psychological damage done since 1972 to their self-confidence and their ability to negotiate with the minority community a new arrangement within Northern Ireland. That, it might be said, is a matter peculiar to the people of Northern Ireland. But the implications of the 1985 Agreement were such that a much greater onus was placed on the British political process than heretofore and it contributed to the developing Anglo-Irish relationship which produced the December 1993 Joint Declaration and the February 1995 Framework Documents. Northern Ireland may be treated as a sideshow by the daily tabloids but cabinet ministers know that it is a matter which can raise its ugly head at any time at their weekly meetings. In other words, while it may not be a matter of continuing debate in academia or the pub, it is a very serious issue in the conduct of every government. This book hopes to draw the salient issues to the attention of a wider audience in the hope that it will stimulate a more informed debate.

We have attempted to provide a thematic investigation of Northern Ireland rather than a purely chronological narrative of the Troubles. The latter can be found in a wide variety of publications, some of which are listed at the end. In chapter 2, however, we discuss the main lines of political developments in the province with particular emphasis on the events of 1968–9, 1974 and since the Anglo-Irish Agreement. Chapter 3 comprises a social and economic analysis, while nationalist and unionist politics – and their relationship with paramilitary activity – are covered in the next two chapters. Security challenges and responses are investigated in chapter 6 and international aspects, especially the burgeoning Anglo-Irish dimension and US involvement, are treated in chapter 7. We conclude with a review of the current peace 'process' and the realistically available policy options.

In writing about Northern Ireland we are sharply aware that language, like everything else in Ireland, has a political dimension. In this respect sensitivity is a key element. The people of Northern Ireland have highly tuned political antennae. Words, accents, even vowels and consonants can convey political flavour. Rather than qualify every sentence in the text, we consider it prudent to announce at the outset that the following clusters will be used without attempting to convey anything sinister or offensive: catholic / nationalist / republican; protestant / unionist/loyalist; Derry / Londonderry (although the particularly sensitive might assert that they should appear in the opposite order); the Irish Republic / Eire / the Republic of Ireland / the South (and for the mathematically inclined 'the twenty-six counties'); similarly Ulster / Northern Ireland / the North / the six counties. All of these can impart a political message which it would be foolhardy to ignore. We try to avoid that trap by being specific in places, but we know that we cannot always get it absolutely right. In any case, to employ these terms without being conscious of their frequently intense political meaning might suggest some form of indifference about the nature of the problem. We hope we are not guilty.

Finally there is the issue of perspective. It takes two forms. One is to state bluntly that it is meaningless to examine developments inside Northern Ireland exclusively since 1968. Our sense of history is profound *and* shallow. Hence, while we are concerned with events since 1968, references to past happenings will be both frequent and necessary. 'History' can be a weapon. The second form concerns the sense of locality and of the individual within that locality, even what some people dismiss disparagingly as 'parochialism'. Undoubtedly it is the case that the level of violent incidents has diminished, especially since the cease fires of August and October 1994. But violence, including 'punishment beatings' and sporadic rioting, still exists, the Troubles have not completely departed, and paramilitarism continues to be a way of life. It is worthwhile reminding ourselves that continuing violence not only diminishes all of us, but can contribute to a sense of hate or despair. Both emotions can fuel further violence.

As an afterword there is need for a health warning: all facts in a volatile political situation speak for themselves when someone gives them the floor. It is the historian who sets the context: others might set different contexts from that which we have chosen, and it is important to remember that virtually every action and every utterance in Northern Ireland can be invested with at least two interpretations.

2 The Northern Ireland Political Landscape

Northern Ireland entered British political consciousness in the summer and autumn of 1968 when there were disturbances in the province following demonstrations sponsored by the Northern Ireland Civil Rights Association (NICRA). NICRA was a broadly based organization in which nationalists, liberal unionists, trade-union activists and other sympathetic parties had joined to press for reform of Northern Ireland's political system. Among their demands was the establishment of 'one-man-one-vote' in local government elections to replace the antiquated businessmen's and ratepayer's franchise which favoured the generally better-off protestant community. They also wanted to sweep away the gerrymandering of local-government boundaries which ensured the unionist domination of many local councils. In Londonderry County Borough in 1967, for example, 14,429 catholic voters (62 per cent of the total) out of 23,210 were able to elect only eight non-unionist councillors out of a total corporation of twenty. Another grievance lay in the discriminatory allocation of public housing. In Dungannon, county Tyrone (an area with a catholic majority), from 1945 to 1968 the local unionist council had allocated nearly three-quarters of the publicly built housing to protestants. It was no accident that the province's first civil rights march was held in the Dungannon area on 24 August 1968.

Although this march passed off relatively peacefully, the second major demonstration, held in Derry on 5 October, was met by a strong contingent of Royal Ulster Constabulary (RUC) ordered in by the Minister of Home Affairs. The march ended with violent clashes and there was rioting throughout the catholic Bogside area of the city during the night that followed. In the autumn, further demonstrations – some which similarly ended in violence – marked the growing vigour of the civil rights movement, which was swelled especially by liberal and radical students from Queen's University in Belfast, attracted by the idealism of the cause and the opportunity it apparently presented for the introduction of 'real' politics in the province in place of the existing tired procedures of sectarian power-broking. NICRA and the student-led 'People's Democracy' (PD) drew inspiration from the contemporary American civil rights movement and also the wave of student unrest which swept across the world in 1968. At the turn of the year a PD march, consciously modelled on Martin Luther King's march from Selma to Montgomery, Alabama, in 1965, set out from Belfast to Derry. But a few miles short of Londonderry on the final day of their march the students were violently attacked by a mob of protestants, including a number of off-duty 'B-Specials', members of the exclusively protestant part-time auxiliary police. Again the Bogside erupted into violence with protestant rioters and some police joining in attacks on the catholics.

Faced with the apparently inexorable escalation of violence, and pressed for action by London, Captain Terence O'Neill, the well-meaning liberal who had been prime minister of the province since 1963, announced a package of reforms which to a very great extent met the original demands of NICRA. But within the unionist community such concessions generated unease and smacked of weakness in the face of violent challenge. Ian Paisley, the extreme evangelical cleric who had for some years been warning of the moral dangers of liberalism in general, caught the mood of many worried unionists when he accused O'Neill of traitorous behaviour. O'Neill, in any case, was not in the same mould as his predecessors. He did not appear to be as deeply rooted in the traditions of the protestant Orange Order and he lacked the common touch, an essential prerequisite in a tightly-knit community. Above all, he was a man with a mission, an innovator who wanted to prepare Northern Ireland for the late twentieth century and its place in the affluent sun. To achieve this a staid and conservative society needed to be shaken up. Besides, the governance of the province was coming under closer scrutiny from Great Britain. Labour, in power since 1964 under Harold Wilson, had little in common with unionism and resented the fact that at a time when Labour had a paper-thin majority Unionist MPs at Westminster voted with the Conservative opposition on matters of no direct concern to Northern Ireland. A backbench pressure group, the Campaign for Democracy in Ulster (CDU), paid close attention to the minority's complaints of discrimination. It had little difficulty in persuading Wilson to put pressure on O'Neill. In any event, the latter may have welcomed Wilson's insistence on reform since it enabled him to unleash an Ulster technocratic version of the 'white heat of the scientific revolution'.

O'Neill's modernization programme had a profound effect within his own community. He attempted to move the levers of power back to the 'centre' at Stormont (where the province's parliament sat) in a society which prided itself on decentralization, on strong local government and on a people who had a clear sense of their own autonomy. Many of them resented notions of centralized planning because it was being imposed by a faceless bureaucracy and was removing what little vestiges of power they felt still remained at local level. Hence Unionist Party revolts in 1966 and 1967 had been as much about the style of O'Neill's leadership as they were with the concessions he appeared to be making to the minority.

As it happened O'Neill's concessions were largely symbolic, if not cosmetic, but they did whet the appetite of the minority's leaders who were much defter than their unionist counterparts in the skills of public relations. Following the election of the Republican Labour candidate, Gerry Fitt, to Westminster in 1966, the minority had a powerful advocate who found a willing audience on the Labour back benches. The result was the introduction of a (muted) reform programme by the Northern Ireland prime minister which angered his more reactionary colleagues and disappointed civil rights activists. In attempting to push through his programme, Captain O'Neill lost four of his cabinet ministers. In response, he called a general election for February 1969 – 'Ulster at the Crossroads'.

O'Neill won, but with a reduced majority and a serious rupture in his party. The impact of that split is still being played out in the unionist community. The impact on the nationalist minority was equally traumatic. The unionist electorate was presented with the opportunity to decide between thirty-nine O'Neill Unionists, seventeen anti-O'Neill Unionist and five Protestant Unionists. It chose twenty-two O'Neillites and eleven anti-O'Neillites. Whereas the Protestant Unionists were unsuccessful on this occasion, their leader, Ian Paisley, performed creditably and his party warmed to the electoral process: within four months he and his deputy were returned to Stormont in by-elections caused by the resignation of Terence O'Neill and a prominent backbencher, Richard Ferguson, following the Unionist Party's acceptance of universal suffrage at local-government level. Ferguson and others from the liberal wing of the Unionist Party later gave support for the bi-communal moderate Alliance Party formed in April 1970. The significance of the February 1969 election for the minority was the challenge to the major opposition Nationalist Party from civil rights activists. Three of them, including John Hume, were elected and they proved to be the nucleus of the Social Democratic and Labour Party (SDLP) formed in August 1970, the most successful nationalist party in the history of Northern Ireland to date. If nothing else, the O'Neill general election radically altered the contours of the political landscape.

O'Neill's departure was assisted by explosions at electrical power installations and a water pipeline in March and April 1960, the handiwork of protestant extremists anxious to help him on his way. His political manner had suggested a more sedate age but his policies had induced a more raucous style of political behaviour. The civil rights campaign, largely based on extraparliamentary activity, produced a strong reaction from a section of the majority community which objected to what it considered a policy of appeasement orchestrated by an alien Labour government in London and carried out by its O'Neillite puppets. Frequent sectarian clashes became the order of the day. Such activity was not unknown in Northern Ireland, but its intensity and consistency after October 1968 gave genuine cause for alarm in Britain where this sort of thing was not expected within the United Kingdom in the late twentieth century.

Westminster and Whitehall's ignorance and innocence were early casualties of 'the Troubles'. Civil servants sent from London to oversee the reform programme took some time to familiarize themselves with the idiosyncracies of the local scene. In particular they worked under the mistaken assumption that they were dealing with a political culture which would be as familiar to them as Surrey or Yorkshire. They were to make the same error as Terence O'Neill in assuming that there were technocratic answers to constitutional conundrums. More importantly, they were unaware of the traditional ambivalence to the political process present in both communities. Obviously they were conscious of recurring street violence and they knew enough history to fear the potential for IRA resurgence. They believed that, at one level, violent political conflict could be resolved by social change. Those who could not be persuaded to enjoy the fruits of a reform programme would constitute a tiny romantic movement which would inevitably wither away. The problem with this approach was that it was based on a rationale which took little account of the longevity and intensity of the quarrel.

This intensity was soon abundantly obvious when very serious violence broke out in the summer of 1969. Faced with quickly escalating riots in Derry and Belfast, where protestant mobs launched savage attacks on catholic areas of west Belfast, the RUC proved unable to cope and O'Neill's successor as prime minister, Major James Chichester-Clark, asked London for the

British army to be deployed on the streets. This was a crucial development. It marked a qualitative change in the nature of the crisis with London becoming more directly involved in the management of the problem. No longer could the violence be dismissed as merely an internal Northern Irish affair. The security arrangements made in the early days, moreover, reflected the haphazard and *ad hoc* nature of British decision-making towards the province. The rapid development of the British army in a 'peacekeeping' role on 15 August 1969 was ordered by London to meet an immediate and urgent crisis. As is often the case in such circumstances, little thought seems to have been given to the long-term implications. In particular, the precise relationship between the military and the police remained unclear. Four days after the troops had been sent in, a joint meeting of representatives from the United Kingdom and Northern Ireland governments at 10 Downing Street, London, agreed that the army General-Officer-Commanding (GOC) would assume 'overall responsibility for security operations'. While remaining answerable 'directly to the Ministry of Defence' (in London), he was to 'work in the closest co-operation with the Northern Ireland Government' and the head of the Royal Ulster Constabulary. For 'normal police duties outside the field of security', the RUC would remain under the direct administration of the Northern Ireland government.

The security chiefs were also subject to local political pressure. The GOC and Chief Constable were both members of a joint security committee which handled general questions of security policy. Chaired by the Northern Ireland Minister of Home Affairs, the committee provided a mechanism for local political and civil service views to be expressed on security matters. On occasions these views vigorously challenged the GOC's opinions. From the start, however, there were difficulties, especially since the problem, and hence the response, was seen rather differently by each interested party. The Northern Ireland government, for example, tended to view the unrest as an IRA-fomented challenge to the state as a whole, while some on the military side believed that both the Belfast administration and the local police themselves had contributed directly to the seriousness of the violence. Thus the central direction of the security effort was flawed. In London the high-level cabinet committee on Northern Ireland did little in the way of policy-making after August 1969. In the words of one of its members it was 'mainly concerned with sorting out the endless disputes between Freeland [the GOC] and the police or between the Ministry of Defence and the Home Office'. One early police-army difference concerned their respective spheres of responsibility as laid down after the Downing Street meeting of 19 August. This was in any case not very satisfactory, since the term 'security operations' was never clearly defined. When Sir Arthur Young, of the City of London Police, was appointed Chief Constable of the RUC in October 1969 he insisted, on the threat of resignation, that the GOC's role be restricted merely to 'co-ordinate' army and police.

There was equal, and growing, uncertainty on the political side. No one was quite sure who was ultimately in charge. London, understandably anxious to keep the whole mess at arm's length, was keen to work through the existing government of Northern Ireland while asserting (if not actually implementing) the sovereignty of the Westminster parliament. This was clearly set out in the 'Downing Street Declaration' of 19 August 1969 which also sought to reassure unionists by reaffirming 'the clear pledges made by successive United Kingdom Governments that Northern Ireland should not cease to be a part of the United Kingdom without the consent of the people of Northern Ireland'. 'The border', it bluntly added, 'is not an issue'. Since 1969, in fact, the British government's policy towards Northern Ireland has been to sub-contract the day-to-day administration of the province on to some local body, while laying down certain minimum political requirements and retaining ultimate control of security.

It was over security matters that the Stormont system finally collapsed. Between the summer of 1969 and the resignation of the Northern Ireland government (by this stage under Brian Faulkner) in March 1972, London steadily expanded its control over security policy. The early reforms insisted upon in 1969 had begun to dismantle the traditional Northern Ireland security apparatus. The B-Specials were disbanded and replaced by the Ulster Defence Regiment (UDR), which although locally raised and mostly part-time was an integral part of the army and thus controlled from London. In July 1992 the UDR was amalgamated with the regular army Royal Irish Rangers and renamed the Royal Irish Regiment. There was also (in 1969–70) a major reform of the RUC, which was disarmed, demilitarized and put under the command of an English policeman, Sir Arthur Young, although notably one with colonial experience. While the police were undergoing this process and recovering from the disasters of 1969, the army assumed the chief role of keeping the peace, yet Stormont still retained a major share in policy-making. In 1970–1, for example, the Northern Ireland government pressed London strongly for the introduction of internment without trial, but when the measure was introduced in August 1971 it turned out to be an unmitigated disaster which was followed by an increase in the level of unrest. The apparently uncontrollable spiral of violence in 1971–2 eventually led Edward Heath to transfer full responsibility for law and order to Westminster. In response Faulkner resigned and direct rule was established with William Whitelaw appointed the first Secretary of State for Northern Ireland.

Whitelaw's great achievement while responsible for Northern Ireland affairs was the creation of the powersharing executive, the most successful of the British political initiatives within the province so far. This initiative, like all others, sought to square the circle of meeting nationalist aspirations without fatally alienating the unionists. The executive, which drew together a group of comparatively moderate unionists, under Brian Faulkner (who became chief executive), the SDLP and the Alliance Party, took office on 1 January 1974 but lasted for just five months. Although candidates favouring powersharing had secured a comfortable majority (fifty out of seventy-eight) in the elections for a local assembly in June 1973, twenty-eight of the fifty unionists returned were resolutely opposed to the idea. In the general election to

Westminster in February 1974, moreover, before the executive had had time to prove itself, eleven out of the twelve Northern Irish seats were won by anti-powersharing unionists fighting together in the United Ulster Unionist Council (UUUC) which secured 51 per cent of the poll. The UUUC claimed that the result was a clear vote of no confidence in Faulkner's executive. Apart from the repugnant notion of sharing power with 'disloyal' members of the minority community, the UUUC took particular exception to the establishment of a Council of Ireland which was supposed to consider matters of common interest, North and South, and to give Dublin a formal – if only consultative – role in the political process.

The UUUC alone did not destroy the executive, but its electoral success legitimized the loyalist protest – the Ulster Workers' Council (UWC) strike of May 1974 – which did. With a combination of disciplined industrial action and open intimidation, the UWC brought the province to a virtual stand-still. This extraparliamentary action was supported by the leading anti-powersharing politicians, such as Ian Paisley and the former Unionist cabinet minister, William Craig, but the real strength of the strike lay with protestant paramilitary organizations: the Ulster Defence Association (UDA), the Ulster Volunteer Force, the Ulster Special Constabulary Association and the Orange Volunteers. The Secretary of State (Merlyn Rees since the February Westminster election) was apparently unwilling to do anything to counter the power of these groups beyond mouthing the usual sort of pious platitudes. Harold Wilson made a broadcast to Northern Ireland in which he called the loyalist strikers 'thugs and bullies' who were 'sponging on British democracy', but he did nothing to match their *force majeure*. British trades-union leaders led an abortive 'back-to-work' march and the security forces remained on the sidelines until near the end of the strike when some moves were begun to mitigate the impact of the stoppage. The UWC's main power lay in its control of the electricity generating industry. The manual workers – mostly protestant – walked out and the white-collar staff, who might have kept a reasonable supply going for at least a limited period, were intimidated into running the system down. As the power cuts got longer and longer the Unionist members of the executive resigned and powersharing collapsed.

The events of May 1974 are crucial to an understanding of the loyalist reaction to the Anglo-Irish Agreement of November 1985. Drawing on the experience of 1974 (and, indeed, on 1912–21 when Irish Home Rule was successfully resisted in Ulster) the loyalist community believed it could literally pull the plug on any political arrangement constructed by the British government which did not suit them. Loyalist reaction to the powersharing executive, moreover, was not only a matter of strikes and demonstrations. During the UWC stoppage car bombs believed to have been planted by protestant extremists exploded in Dublin and Monaghan in the Republic, killing twenty-seven people. Loyalist terrorists, though much less active than republican, have also played a significant role in the Troubles, especially at times of political uncertainty – 1969, 1974 or in the aftermath of the Anglo-Irish Agreement.

After the fall of the powersharing executive, the 1970s can be seen as a period of political stalemate. While the British government remained wedded to the notion of powersharing, it was unable to persuade the Northern Ireland political parties to agree to implement such an arrangement. A Constitutional Convention set up in May 1975 was dominated by loyalist intransigents who formulated a scheme which effectively called for the restoration of the Stormont system and specifically rejected powersharing at cabinet level. London refused to accept this proposal and dissolved the Convention in March 1976. Both Roy Mason (Secretary of State 1976–9) and Humphrey Atkins (1979–81) introduced 'initiatives' which led to inconclusive talks with the local political parties. In each case the refusal of unionists to contemplate full powersharing proved to be an insuperable stumbling-block. And as successive British attempts to secure an internal settlement failed, the SDLP increasingly began to look south for a way out of the imbroglio.

So, in fact, did London. An important development of British policy towards Northern Ireland has been the growing belief in London that the Irish government must play a central part in *any* resolution of the conflict. Anglo-Irish relations were poor, to say the least, in the early 1970s. The apparent inability of the British government to control the escalating violence was widely criticized in the Republic. The events of 'Bloody Sunday', 20 January 1972, when British soldiers shot dead thirteen unarmed men during a demonstration in Derry, particularly inflamed sections of Southern opinion. An angry crowd marched on the British Embassy in Dublin and burnt it down. But the Northern Ireland troubles also posed a threat to the peace and stability of the Republic, and the possibility of both loyalist and republican violence spreading south of the border was shockingly brought home to the Southerners by the bombs of May 1974, the assassination of Christopher Ewart-Biggs, the British Ambassador to the Republic, in July 1976, and the killing of Lord Mountbatten near his county Sligo holiday home in August 1979. Dublin's wish to secure a peaceful solution to the Northern Ireland conflict is underpinned by the growing economic burden of maintaining a heightened security effort and an appreciation of the challenge – largely irrelevant to the everyday concerns of the Republic – posed to the Southern political system by extreme republicanism.

Such considerations have led successive Irish governments to participate in a process which led to the Anglo-Irish Agreement of November 1985. This process began in May 1980 when Mrs Thatcher and Charles Haughey, the Irish Taoiseach (prime minister), reached agreement on 'new and close political co-operation'. A few days later the chief constable of the RUC and the Garda (Irish police) Commissioner met for the first time to discuss improved cross-border security arrangements. At the end of the year Thatcher and Haughey met again and agreed to establish Anglo-Irish studies on matters of common concern. In a significant phrase, the two prime ministers contemplated an examination of 'the totality of relationships within these islands'. The joint studies reported in November 1981 and recommended, among other things, the establishment of an 'Intergovernmental Council' of ministers to review Anglo-Irish policy towards Northern Ireland.

In 1981 and 1982, however, Anglo-Irish relations were at times very strained. Dublin was sharply critical of Mrs Thatcher's handling of the republican hunger strikes in 1981, and the 'H-block' campaign (named after the shape of the buildings in the Maze Prison) in support of the strikers was able to mobilize opinion in the Republic – so much so that two hunger strikers were elected to the Dail (Dublin parliament) in the general election of June 1981. In the spring of the following year Mr Haughey's criticism of British policy towards the Argentine occupation of the Falklands led to a diplomatic estrangement with Mrs Thatcher which was not repaired until November 1983, a year after Garrett FitzGerald had succeeded Haughey as Taoiseach.

Meanwhile the British government once more turned its attention to the possibility of an internal solution in Northern Ireland. In the autumn of 1982 a new Assembly was established to which, it was hoped, responsibilities for local affairs could progressively be transferred from the Whitehall Northern Ireland Office. This idea of 'rolling devolution' depended, however, on a measure of agreement – which did not emerge – between the main political parties. The SDLP, while fighting the elections for the Assembly, boycotted its meetings on the grounds that a purely internal settlement was no longer viable. Without SDLP participation the initiative could never amount to much. The unionist parties and Alliance co-operated in developing some scrutinizing functions for the Assembly, but no scheme for powersharing which could include the SDLP was agreed. In the absence of any such proposal the Assembly lapsed into no more than an expensive and futile talking-shop. It was finally dissolved on 23 June 1986.

The re-establishment of friendly relations between Dublin and London which Garrett FitzGerald earnestly desired was marked by the summit meeting with the British prime minister in November 1983, after which the intergovernmental council commenced operating. Between November 1983 and March 1985 the council met thirty times and paved the way for the Anglo-Irish Agreement signed at Hillsborough Castle, county Down (the Secretary of State's official residence), on 15 November 1985. By formalizing the joint efforts of the British and Irish governments to secure reconciliation in Northern Ireland, the Agreement provided unequivocal acceptance that the problem was a joint one. In order to reassure the Northern unionists, Article I contained the two governments' affirmation 'that any change in the status of Northern Ireland would only come about with the consent of a majority of the people of Northern Ireland'. But, to the unionists' horror, Dublin was given a consultative role as of right regarding policy in the North. Within the framework of the intergovernmental council, Article 2 provided that an intergovernmental conference would be convened regularly to consider '(i) political matters; (ii) security and related matters; (iii) legal matters, including the administration of justice; (iv) the promotion of cross-border co-operation'. The bulk of the Agreement outlined what was to be the role of the conference with special reference to these four matters. It was to be serviced by a secretariat composed of senior officials from London and Dublin based at Maryfield, outside Belfast. The secretariat was to act as a channel of communication between the governments, but not as a decision-making body.

The Agreement received a very wide welcome in Britain, Ireland and internationally. The House of Commons ratified it with an overwhelming majority of 426. In the Dail the vote was much closer – 88 to 75 – although still clearly in favour. The Agreement was registered with the United Nations and favourably received by President Reagan and the US Congress. International goodwill also came from all major West European states, the EEC, and from Canada, Australia and New Zealand. The importance of the international dimension was recognized in the Agreement itself. Article 10(a) saw the potential of promoting economic and social development to regenerate a depressed local economy by considering 'the possibility of international support'. The US, Canada and New Zealand contributed to an International Fund and, although the sums donated were relatively small (the US giving $120 million over three years), the contributions have considerable symbolic significance as an indication of international goodwill.

Apart from the guarantee that the constitutional status of Northern Ireland would not be altered without the consent of the population, the framers of the Agreement hoped to deflect unionist opposition by building in considerable flexibility – some would say 'ambiguity' – to the operation of the conference. The intention was to make the conference unboycottable, if not impervious to criticism. In the first instance local politicians were not to be involved in its workings. Yet Articles 4(b), 5(c) and 10(b) were designed to act as catalysts towards achieving powersharing devolution within the province in place of an *enhanced* role for the conference.

But the unionists responded to the Agreement with very bitter and sustained opposition. 'We are going to be delivered, bound and trussed like a turkey ready for the oven, from one nation to another nation', declared James Molyneaux, the leader of the Ulster Unionist Party (UUP), to a special sitting of the Northern Ireland Assembly the day after the Agreement had been signed. A massive loyalist demonstration on 23 November 1985 brought Belfast city centre to a standstill when a crowd, estimated at between 50,000 and 100,000 (over 10 per cent of the *entire* protestant population), proclaimed its profound opposition to the measure. A *Sunday Times* opinion poll the following day found 49 per cent of protestants opposed to the Agreement with only 14 per cent in favour. Beyond the loyalist gut reaction against the deal, however, the unionist community has been unable to devise any clear and satisfactory strategy to destroy, or even amend, the Agreement. While James Molyneaux and the Democratic Unionist Party (DUP) leader Ian Paisley attempted to control and lead reaction through street demonstrations, Westminster and local-government boycotts, and a muted campaign of civil disobedience, some of the secondary leadership moved off on disparate paths.

Some toyed with forms of independence, while others, such as the Campaign for Equal Citizenship, pressed for the integration of Northern Ireland within the United Kingdom generally. They argued that if the 'national' parties organized in the province, as elsewhere in the UK, this would enable the removal of sectarianism from local politics. The leader of this group, Robert McCartney, a prominent unionist QC, stood on an 'equal citizenship' ticket in the June 1987 Westminster general election and polled 14,467 votes in the North Down constituency. In the same election, however, one of the leading integrationists, Enoch Powell, lost his seat to the SDLP. An alternative option was mapped out by the Charter Group, led by the former Stormont cabinet minister Harry West, which opposed administrative devolution and sought regional autonomy. Of the two main unionist parties, the DUP was more resolute in its opposition to the Agreement and adopted a more militant line which set the tone for its extraparliamentary campaign, much of it to the embarrassment of the UUP. Violence, for example, occurred outside Maryfield on 11 December 1985 and 4 January 1986, in various parts of the province following a 'day of action' on 3 March 1986 and in Portadown in March and July. On the first anniversary of the signing of the Agreement two people died and seventy were injured following loyalist demonstrations. In Belfast city centre over seventy shops were damaged, and some looted, after a mass protest around the city hall. Supporters of the UUP, more traditionally conservative and law-abiding than their DUP colleagues, have been disturbed by the violence accompanying opposition to the Agreement, especially attacks on the RUC. The level of violence has generally increased in the post-Agreement period. Fatal casualties rose by 21 per cent in 1986, and the total for the whole year had already been exceeded by the end of August 1987. Much of the increase was due to a sharp rise in loyalist paramilitarism in its campaign against the Agreement. Equally disturbing was the rise in the level of intimidation: at the end of 1986 the Housing Executive reported that it had dealt with 1,118 cases of families driven from their homes, almost all the result of loyalist paramilitaries attacking the houses of catholics or members of the RUC.

By mid-1987 explicit unionist opposition to the Anglo-Irish Agreement had somewhat declined. Unionist local councils were returning to normal activity. High hopes had been entertained that the United Kingdom general election in June might produce a 'hung' parliament in which the unionist MPs (as in 1977–9) could exert a disproportionate influence. Mrs Thatcher's clear victory, however, left the unionists with no specific policy beyond opposition to the Agreement. This unsettled many unionist supporters and there was evidence of continuing rifts within the unionist family, including resignations of some younger active members of both parties who have apparently been frustrated by the negativism of party policy. Under the Anglo-Irish Agreement (Article 11) there was to be a review by November 1988. That brought little comfort to unionists when it reported in May 1989. Instead it underlined the durability of the Agreement by concentrating on increased functional co-operation. The penultimate paragraph held out the prospect for some change.

> If in future it were to appear that the objectives of the Agreement could be more effectively served by changes in the scope and nature of the working of the Conference, consistent with the basic provisions and spirit of the Agreement, the two Governments would be ready in principle to consider such changes.

This offered unionists some scope to re-enter the political process within the ambit of the Anglo-Irish framework. We shall see how they measured up to that challenge in chapter 8.

3   A Place Apart

In 1976 the well-known Irish travel writer Dervla Murphy, who had published celebrated accounts of her bicycle journeys to India and other remote parts, toured Northern Ireland for the first time. The outcome of her visit was a brilliant and compassionate book, *A Place Apart*, which provides one of the best possible introductions to the communities and psychology of the North. Before her journey Dervla Murphy, who comes from county Waterford in the south-east corner of Ireland, had shared with many of her compatriots a fixed view of Northern Ireland as a peculiar place, mainly populated by irrational and violent people, which although lying within the island of Ireland is a very different and distinct locality. But Northern Ireland is a place apart not only in Ireland but also in the United Kingdom. Nearly seventy years of separate administration coupled with twenty five years of communal unrest, moreover, have exacerbated these differences and enhanced its 'apartness'. Yet the north of Ireland has always had a particularity all of its own, in religious, social, economic and even national terms. It must also be borne in mind that Northern Ireland is an extremely parochial place and one result of the Troubles has been to make it more so. Matters of life and death have forced people to fall back on their own resources and to close ranks. The proximity both of the communities to each other and of politicians to the people they represent has enormously enhanced the primacy of specifically local issues and tragically reduced the capability of politicians of one tradition to empathize with their colleagues of the other.

The Northern Ireland conflict is frequently characterized as a religious one. In a technical sense this is not true. Although religious observance and churchgoing remain at a higher level in the province than in the rest of the United Kingdom, people in Northern Ireland are not fighting about theological points such as transubstantiation, predestination or papal infallibility. The leaders of the mainstream Christian denominations have consistently deplored the use of violence in the province and the frequent condemnation of violence by the catholic hierarchy, including the Pope during his visit to Ireland in 1979, make it absurd to suppose that members of the IRA, for example, are in any way expressing catholic *religious* opinion. Nevertheless religion remains a key social and political determinant in the province. It is not a question of religious belief but one of social and political identification. Put simply, most unionists are to be found in the protestant community and most nationalists in the catholic one. To a very great extent, and increasingly so since the Troubles began, catholics and protestants live in separate areas, they are educated apart and develop distinct cultural identities.

In general the self-perception of the protestant is one of 'British' nationality, loyalty to the British Crown and a commitment to the kinds of civil and political liberties established in Britain by the events of the seventeenth century, particularly the 'Glorious Revolution' of 1688. Although in Great Britain the political significance of the exclusively protestant nature of the British monarchy, as established in 1688, has largely disappeared, in Northern Ireland it remains a crucial component of the Ulster protestant's loyalty to the British Crown. The Ulster 'loyalist' is, above all, a protestant loyalist. For the catholic it is rather different. Irish nationality is combined with a history of national and religious subordination to 'English imperialism' and a heritage of the partially successful struggle for Irish freedom. For some catholics (although only a tiny minority of the total) the IRA campaign is simply the contemporary expression of that continuing battle.

Given that political attitudes and religious identification roughly coincide, then the communal 'numbers game' in Northern Ireland assumes a very great importance. Successive guarantees by the British government that the constitutional status of Northern Ireland can be changed only with the agreement of a majority of the population, and similar assurances contained in the Anglo-Irish Agreement and the Joint Declaration, mean that the relative size of the two communities – and potential changes therein – is of vital significance.

According to the 1991 census (which is generally regarded as being accurate) catholics now constitute 42 per cent of the 1.58 million population – a figure which rises to 53 per cent for the under-sixteens. A closer examination of the statistics reveal several worrying features for the protestant majority. According to 'The Numbers Game', a series of programmes presented on Ulster Television in August 1994, the protestant heartland is diminishing. Belfast now has a 45 per cent catholic population, and certain unionist wards are becoming 'marginals'. In greater Belfast in what was predominantly an area of staunch loyalism, Lisburn District Council, 43 per cent of the school going population are catholics. One reason may be the overspill from Belfast: when the Twinbrook estate was built in 1971 it had fifteen families – by 1994 7,500 catholics resided there. Some would assert that the border has 'moved' in places: in Newry and Mourne district, for example, the young protestant population is down to below 20 per cent so that Banbridge town has become a sort of new 'front line'.

These figures need to be treated with some caution. It is true that the catholic proportion of the population has increased over the years. In the mid-1920s 33.7 per cent of the population were catholic. Geographically they were concentrated in the south and west of the province and in west Belfast. As we have seen, the latest figures suggest that there are fewer areas where they are not well represented. Traditionally, however, high rates of catholic emigration have restricted the growth of that population. Nevertheless, it has been calculated that between 1961 and 1981 the catholic population grew ten times faster than the non-catholic. Whether this trend will ineluctably continue until catholics achieve a numerical majority is of real political concern. But it should not be exaggerated. For unionist politicians the real worry is about the loss of *local* control in areas where there has been a demographic shift.

There is – or should be – less concern about Northern Ireland's constitutional status since the signing of the Joint Declaration. The opening sentence of paragraph 4 reads: 'The Prime Minister, on behalf of the British Government, reaffirms that they will uphold the democratic wish of the greater number of the people of Northern Ireland, on the issue of whether they prefer to support the Union or a sovereign united Ireland'. In turn paragraph 5 [in part] reads, on behalf of the Irish government: '. . . it would be wrong to attempt to impose a united Ireland, in the absence of the freely given consent of a majority of the people of Northern Ireland'. In other words the new vocabulary has shifted from old fashioned (unionist) majoritarianism to the doctrine of consent. Persuasion rather than coercion belongs to the new order.

Education is an area of marked segregation between catholics and protestants in Northern Ireland. Early in its life the unionist government at Stormont introduced an education act aimed at establishing an essentially secular, publicly-funded system of primary education throughout the province. But there was such strong opposition from both the catholic and the protestant churches (who wish to retain control over education) that the government was obliged to drop the measure. Although the amended act asserted that the state education system should be non-sectarian, it also stipulated (as was the case elsewhere in the United Kingdom) that Christian religious education be included in the syllabus. To qualify for a full government subsidy, however, a school had to provide distinctively protestant 'Bible teaching'. In effect this meant that the state primary-education system was a protestant one. A similar state of affairs obtained after 1947 when the Northern Ireland government, following the British Butler Education Act of 1944, introduced free secondary education for all so long as they stayed within the state sector but still restricted the assistance available for the province's specifically denominational (mostly catholic) schools. Since the late 1960s, a series of changes begun under Captain O'Neill have increased government subsidies for denominational schools and the catholic sector is now much less disadvantaged than before. But at the primary and secondary levels most children in Northern Ireland are still educated in religiously segregated institutions. Since 1981 when Lagan College opened there has been a sustained push towards encouraging integrated education. In 1989 a formal statutory provision was introduced to make state funding available for the establishment of new integrated schools and to facilitate the conversion of existing schools to integrated status. Currently there are 17 integrated primary schools and four secondary-level colleges with a further two colleges starting in September 1994. Nonetheless there are just under 4,000 pupils out of a total of 335,00 being educated in an integrated environment; and in the state sector catholics remain at under 10 per cent. Teacher training is similarly divided and will remain so for the foreseeable future. These educational divisions have considerable social repercussions although they are as much a product of a divided community as a cause.

The situation is much more satisfactory in further and higher education which is almost totally integrated. The 1947 Education Act provided for grant-aided university education which gave new opportunities especially to catholic students, and facilitated the growth of a catholic professional class which in turn played a significant role in the development of the civil rights movement. The government funding for education at all levels in Northern Ireland has been rather more generous than anything available in the Republic. It is, ironically, currently cheaper in terms of fees for Southern students to come to university in the North than to stay at home, since under EEC regulations the British government is obliged to charge all EEC nationals at the same rate as home students.

Since the end of the Second World War social policies in Northern Ireland have gone 'step by step' with those in Great Britain. The welfare reforms of the wartime coalition and the postwar Attlee government were matched by similar measures in the province. But since Northern Ireland could not afford to fund these developments out of its own exchequer, Westminster has had to provide an annual subvention. In this, of course, Northern Ireland is no different from any other poor part of the United Kingdom except that with a separate exchequer the Treasury subvention is easier to calculate than otherwise. In 1992–3 the subvention to Northern Ireland amounted to over £3,000 million, some 45 per cent of the total annual public expenditure.

The 1993 Family Expenditure Survey supplies data on differences within Northern Ireland and between the province and the rest of the UK. The average gross weekly income for Northern Ireland's households is 17 per cent lower than in the UK as a whole although that gap is narrowing: the difference in 1990 was 31 per cent. Two other regions – the North (of England) and the West Midlands – are worse off than Northern Ireland. But the financial gap between catholic and protestant households is getting wider with catholics 17 per cent worse off than protestants: 29 per cent of catholic households depend on social security for their income as opposed to 17 per cent of protestants. In relation to public spending on the island of Ireland as a whole the gap is narrowing. During 1993 the authorities responsible for social security benefits in Belfast and Dublin collaborated in a production of a publication which compared the social security benefits in both parts of Ireland. Their findings were published as an annex to a Report from an Economic and Social Affairs Committee of the British-Irish Inter-Parliamentary Body in April 1994.

In the past the north-east of Ireland was also very distinct in economic terms for it was the only part of the island fully to experience nineteenth-century industrialization comparable to that occurring in Great Britain. The development of factory-based textile (mostly linen) production, engineering concerns, and in Belfast a world-scale shipbuilding industry marked Ulster out from the rest of Ireland, which lacked the basic raw materials – coal and iron ore – for an industrial revolution. Easy sea communications here worked in Ulster's favour, with coal and iron efficiently and economically being supplied from north-west England and south-west Scotland. Much of the risk capital for industrial development in the province came from Great Britain, and the customers for Ulster's industrial products were also British. It was Glasgow and Liverpool concerns, not Dublin or Cork, who purchased the ships built by the great Belfast yard of Harland & Wolff. The emergence of large-scale Ulster resistance to Home Rule in the late nineteenth century came at a time when, as never before, the economic and commercial prosperity of the region seemed to depend on the maintenance of close political links with Great Britain.

Today, in much less prosperous times, Northern Ireland's economic survival also seems to depend on the continuance of the union. Ulster was one of the last parts of the United Kingdom to industrialize and it was among the first to begin to experience the economic decline which has afflicted much of the country's traditional industries. With a brief respite during the Second World War, Northern Ireland has suffered high levels of unemployment since the 1920s. In August 1987 unemployment, which during the 1980s had exceeded 20 per cent, stood at over 18 per cent, in comparison to the United Kingdom's average of 10 per cent. In the 1990s it rarely fell below 14 per cent, a figure which dropped to 12.8 per cent in June 1994, its lowest level for three years. The old staple industries have greatly declined. Harland & Wolff, which had 26,000 employees in Belfast in 1945, employed fewer than 2,000 fifty years later. Between 1969 and 1995 the total numbers employed in manufacturing industry fell from 177,000 to just over 100,000.

The existence of long-term structural unemployment has serious social implications, and successive Northern Irish administrations have made great efforts to reduce it. Employment in traditional textile manufacturing, which fell by 23,000 in the 1960s when the linen industry was in steep decline, was partly replaced by 10,000 new jobs in an expanding man-made-fibres industry, attracted to the province in part by government incentives. But the oil crisis of the 1970s, which sharply pushed up raw-material costs for synthetic-textile manufacturers, the civil disorders and world over-capacity led to the closure of many factories. The provision of subsidies, purpose-built factories, interest-free loans and other assistance through the Industrial Development Board (IDB) and the Local Enterprise Development Unit remains a central part of the government's economic strategy. Harland & Wolff, for example, only survived with a substantial government subsidy, which amounted to £68 million in 1986; in the meantime it has been privatised. The government's efforts to attract foreign investment have met with mixed fortunes. The understandable anxiety of politicians and officials to secure major industrial projects has led to serious misjudgements, such as in the case of the De Lorean Motor Company which collapsed in 1982 leaving debts of over £100 million.

There are some relatively healthy manufacturing concerns in Northern Ireland. These include Short Brothers, the aircraft and missile manufacturer – now owned by the Canadian company Bombardier – which is the province's largest single private employer with over 9,000 employees. Quality Irish linen is still produced, though in limited quantities, and there is a successful clothing industry which includes some major suppliers for the retailers Marks and Spencer. There has, too, been recent expansion in pharmaceutical manufacturing and electronics. But the manufacturing sector as a whole represents only 16 per cent of Northern Ireland's Gross Domestic Product.

By contrast, the public sector dominates economic activity in the province, accounting, for example, for 35 per cent of all employment, much of which is directly related to the Troubles. It has been calculated roughly that some 20,000 security-related jobs may be lost if the cessation of violence becomes permanent. These losses may be offset by increased inward investment and above all an expansion of tourism, long deterred by the continuation of violence. Yet even in peaceful circumstances the economic challenges facing Northern Ireland will remain very considerable indeed. Further government encouragement for industrial investment, and large-scale public sector employment, seem essential, but innovative and imaginative ventures, such as the development of a Belfast–Dublin economic 'growth corridor', jointly proposed by the Confederation of British Industry and the Irish Business and Employers' Confederation in 1994, will also have to play a part.

Employment in itself, however, is not enough: the communal impact of job-creation has to be addressed. Historically protestants in Northern Ireland have found it easier than catholics to get jobs, and this has been regarded as part of the general pattern of discrimination which the minority community has suffered. Short Brothers' main factory, for example, is located in east Belfast – hard loyalist territory – and the workforce is predominantly protestant with a long tradition of militant unionism which it shares with the workers at the neighbouring Harland and Wolff shipyard. The company has been one of the targets of a campaign led by Irish-American republican sympathizers – the Irish National Caucus – to take action against Northern Irish firms which are perceived as discriminating against the minority. Shorts, who do much business with the USA – among other things they are a subcontractor for Boeing – were understandably anxious not to jeopardize this work, but traditional employment patterns and the location of the factory made it difficult to make quick changes. Nevertheless, the expansion of operations into part of the former De Lorean car plant in west Belfast, and the active recruitment of catholics, has started to alter the composition of the workforce.

US pressure for change in the employment area coalesced around the so-called MacBride principles, approved by Sean MacBride, an IRA leader between the wars, Irish Foreign Minister 1948–51 and later a senior United Nations diplomat who won the 1974 Nobel Peace Prize and the 1977 Lenin Peace Prize. These principles comprise a series of guidelines for equal-opportunity work practices, including increased job opportunities for 'under-represented religious groups in the workforce' (effectively catholics), adequate security for minority employees, the prohibition of provocative sectarian symbols from the workplace and the abolition of employment criteria based on religious affiliation. This campaign, which was linked to one calling for disinvestment from South Africa, has met with some success in the United States, despite the strenuous opposition of the British government, the leader of the SDLP, John Hume, and the American government. Legislation was adopted in New York, for example, preventing any state pension fund from investing in US companies in Northern Ireland which are judged to be guilty of discrimination. US investment is very important to the province. A number of major concerns, such as Ford and Du Pont Chemicals, have branches here and these companies are certainly susceptible to shareholder pressure back home.

Three main objections have been levied against the MacBride principles. In the first place the positive discrimination in favour of catholics envisaged by the principles would be illegal under current Northern Ireland legislation. The Fair Employment Act 1976 made it unlawful for an employer to discriminate in the selection of an employee on the grounds of religious belief or political opinion. Secondly it has been asserted that the MacBride principles present a deceptively and dangerously simple answer to a very complicated problem. Applied enthusiastically by distant external activists, whose motives may not always be limited merely to an improvement in employment practices, the principles take little account of the complexities of the situation in Northern Ireland and in the end may make it more difficult to arrive at a satisfactory internal resolution of the problem. In the third place the principles have been characterized as counter-productive. Their impact may be actually to curtail US investment in Northern Ireland and thus reduce job opportunities all round. This, indeed, is the main consideration underlying the SDLP's doubts about the principles.

Yet the problem of continuing catholic disadvantage is a very real one as the figures from the 1993 Family Expenditure Survey show. Measured by a variety of social indexes, the catholic community remains underprivileged in comparison with the protestant. The areas of greatest unemployment tend to be in predominantly catholic districts in the south and west of the province. Although there have been improvements in the position of employed catholics these have occurred from a comparatively low base. Hence in March 1994 the Chairman of the Fair Employment Commission (FEC), Bob Cooper, reported 'significant progress' in combatting religious discrimination but added: 'On the face of it we are almost one-third of the way along the road to the elimination of the deficit'. We can trace this tortuous progress through census figures and other reports. Between the 1971 and 1981 censuses, for example, the number of catholics who were 'managers of large establishments' more than doubled, while the protestant figure increased by just over half. More than a decade later the percentage of catholics as managers and in the professions has risen by three and four respectively. Catholic employment had improved generally from 32 to 34 per cent, and more than 41 per cent of new male recruits in the private sector were catholics. In the Northern Ireland Civil Service catholic numbers had increased by one fifth between 1980–85; and by 1994 they represented almost 37 per cent of the 30,000 strong workforce, an increase by more than two per cent over the last six years. Despite this improvement, the representation of each community at different levels of the service remains asymmetrical.

Clearly there is much to be done. A start has been made with the introduction of fair employment legislation. Despite the existence of the Fair Employment Agency (established under 1976 legislation) with a specific brief to promote equitable employment practices, change has occurred only very slowly, especially in the private sector. During the 1980s the emphasis shifted from individual complaints of discrimination against employers to external monitoring and more general investigations of patterns of employment in major sectors or firms. In response to this approach, and to the growing impact of the MacBride campaign, in September 1987 the government announced the introduction of a new code of practice to counter discrimination, and in the 1989 Fair Employment Act replaced the Fair Employment Agency with the more powerful Fair Employment Commission and a Fair Employment Tribunal to consider complaints. The current code recommends that employers advertise vacancies widely, rather than relying on word-of-mouth recruitment. It deplores the preferential treatment of existing employees' relatives, and urges the removal of qualifications or conditions of employment which are not job-related, such as service in the armed forces. The government is pledged to refuse to do business with anyone who does not comply with the code and since it is far and away the largest employer and placer of contracts in the province, this represents a substantial sanction, and now embraces 92 public sector bodies and 3,814 private companies with more than 11 workers each.

The 'apartness' of the Northern Irish communities in religious, social, educational, economic and even geographical terms is very deep-rooted indeed. Nearly twenty years of communal – frequently sectarian – violence has served to deepen many of the divisions. The Troubles have also tended to confirm a 'partition mentality', both north and south of the border. For unionists, republican terrorism has merely confirmed their fear and dislike of the South, a state of mind which emerged very clearly indeed in the near-hysterical reaction to the Anglo-Irish Agreement and the more muted, though still deeply suspicious response to the Framework Documents nearly ten years later. Ironically, for many Southern people the troubles have also confirmed partition. Many parlour nationalists who formerly would have paid lip service to the ideal of a united Ireland now positively reject that option, since it would, they believe, destructively incorporate in any new Irish state a million embittered and dangerous protestants. There is a marked contrast between these partitionist attitudes and the perception of British and Irish politicians that the difficulties of Northern Ireland can only be mitigated by closer co-operation between London, Dublin and both communities in the North. While the people of Ireland, North and South, have apparently moved further apart, the governments which represent the national aspirations of the differing communities in these islands have moved closer together. Therein lies one of the many curious paradoxes of contemporary Northern Irish history.

4 Unionist Politics

Northern Ireland was dominated by the Unionists from its foundation in 1921. Until 1969 all general elections had an unerring and deadening predictability. The reasons were simple. The first-past-the-post electoral system encouraged strong single-party government, and, in a polity in which religious affiliation was the chief voting determinant, the protestant majority voted overwhelmingly for the Unionist Party. There was little choice. The opposition parties were fragmented and frustrated, devoid of proper organization and lacking an attractive and positive programme. As often as not, seats were uncontested: from 1929 to 1969 inclusive 37.5 per cent of all seats went unopposed, and in a fifty-two seat lower house Unionists never held fewer than thirty-two.

It was not that the Unionist Party displayed obvious electoral verve or that in government it was particularly dynamic. On the contrary, it threw up very few politicians of real calibre – unlike many MPs from Scotland and Wales, no Ulster Unionist at Westminster was of sufficient stature to find a place in the cabinet. Equally, the government of Northern Ireland was no better than mediocre during this period. If the ability to stamp one's authority on the whole community and to command its respect is the hallmark of good and successful government, then (as events after 1969 demonstrated) Unionist government did not pass muster. It perceived its role as looking after the interests of the majority community and it did little in the way of attempting to woo the minority. Its record in respect of the former was clearly good enough to ensure those predictable electoral results.

Unionist success was built on a combination of the politics of patronage and its recurrent attempts at raising the spectre of nationalist domination. In a society of limited resources, it could not always guarantee the good life for its own supporters, but it could (and did) frequently raise emotions. It has to be said that there were some grounds for invoking fear. After all, the unionist population, one million at most, shared the island with a nationalist majority. The minority of that majority, about 500,000 people, were considered as fifth columnists residing within the territory, and the remainder belonged to a hostile state which made irredentist claims on Northern Ireland. It was, and is, written into the (1937) Constitution of the Irish Republic:

Art. 2   The national territory consists of the whole island of Ireland, its islands and territorial seas.

Art. 3   Pending the re-integration of the national territory and without prejudice to the right of the Parliament and Government established by this Constitution to exercise jurisdiction over the whole of that territory, the laws enacted by that Parliament shall have the like area and extent of application as the laws of Saorstat Eireann [i.e. over the twenty-six counties only] and the like extra-territorial effect.

Unionists, moreover, were conscious of the physical threat posed by the IRA. That organization was implacable in its opposition to partition and was prepared to adopt any means to dismantle the border and impose Irish unity.

In these circumstances 'eternal vigilance' was the watchword of the majority, and its style of government laid heavy emphasis on security and on the dire necessity of keeping the ship of state afloat. Radical policies in any shape or form were to be eschewed as Northern Ireland basked in its self-induced image as a peaceful but provincial backwater. The unionist tradition, thus, draws on a heritage of both confident supremacy, based on its majority position in Northern Ireland and its ability, as in 1912–21, to mobilize powerful allies in Westminster, and perpetual siege, with its precious protestant community (and state) under threat both from the disloyal minority within the province and the apparently priest-ridden Irish Republic. The events of 1969 and after merely confirmed to convinced unionists like Paisley and many others the error of O'Neill's absurd woolly liberalism and exposed the reality of the continued threat to the very existence of Northern Ireland.

Unionists, too, have experienced a growing lack of confidence in Britain's determination to nourish the union: hence the imposition of direct rule in 1972 found a former Unionist cabinet minister, William Craig, asserting that the Ulster loyalists were 'an old and historic community' for whom union with Britain had never been 'an end in itself' but 'was always a means of preserving Ulster's British tradition and the identity of her Loyalist people'. Loyalty, therefore, took on a specific meaning so that one's primary identity was to the people and territory of Northern Ireland rather than the United Kingdom of Great Britain and Northern Ireland. One even finds a former prime minister, Lord Brookeborough, exclaiming: 'Since I've become an Ulsterman I hate the English rather more' (quoted in W. Van Voris, *Violence in Ulster: An Oral Documentary*, University of Massachusetts Press, 1975, p. 4). Such exclusiveness fails to fulfil one of the criteria for membership of the United Kingdom as laid down by a former Home Secretary, Reginald Maudling, 'that the overall authority of the Westminster parliament was recognised as in the rest of the United Kingdom' (*Memoirs*, Sidgwick and Jackson, 1978, p. 187).

Clearly, that was not the case every time Ulster loyalism faced a constitutional crisis. It was not true in 1912–14 during the Home Rule crisis; nor was it the case between 1920 and 1922 when the constitutional identity of Northern Ireland was under threat. And we shall see that as events unfolded after 1972 Ulster's loyalty was again called into question. Maudling's second criterion, that United Kingdom standards of political behaviour were accepted, was blatantly ignored time after time. To the outside world Ulster loyalism appeared strident, sectarian, aggressive and exclusivist. The paramilitary was to conduct his own brand of politics but the politician was not slow to call on the paramilitary when the times demanded. There was open collaboration during the Ulster Workers' Council (UWC) strike in May 1974 and again during the 1977 'constitutional stoppage'. Cohabitation between the paramilitaries and the politicians was resurrected in the 1980s with the creation of the 'Third Force' in 1981 (following the Anglo-Irish summit of December 1980), and of the Ulster Clubs and Ulster Resistance in the run-up to and aftermath of the signing of the Anglo-Irish Agreement. Paramilitaries had played an important role in resisting Home Rule after 1912 – although then their political masters, Sir Edward Carson and Sir James Craig, preferred to see them as an unofficial or 'provisional' army. This 'army', the Ulster Volunteer Force (UVF), moreover, had the support of many leading British Tories at that time. However, with the securing of Northern Ireland and its seeming legitimation the latterday UVF became something of an embarrassment. It re-formed in 1966 at a time of protestant working-class discontent with the prime minister's liberalizing policies and shot dead a young catholic outside a pub in the Shankill district of Belfast. Captain O'Neill promptly proscribed the organization.

The most obvious distinction between the two communities in their relationship with their 'own' paramilitaries is that loyalist paramilitaries have had a woeful record on those occasions when they have contested elections. The Vanguard Unionist Party (VUP), founded and led by the former Home Affairs Minister, William Craig, in March 1973, sat on the Ulster Loyalist Central Co-ordinating Committee along with representatives of the paramilitary Ulster Defence Association (UDA) and many of those shop stewards who initiated the UWC strike in 1974. Vanguard won seven seats (out of seventy-eight) in the Northern Ireland Assembly elections in March 1973. That increased to fourteen in 1975 but within a year the party had declined to a rump, split on whether it should temporarily share power with the SDLP. In 1979 its last elected representative, William Craig, lost his Westminster seat. Another example is that of the Volunteer Political Party, the political wing of the UVF, formed in April 1974, shortly after the UVF had been 'deproscribed'. Its chairman, Ken Gibson, contested the October 1974 Westminster election but took only 2,690 votes, one in seven of the protestant vote. That appeared to be the end of that particular party and within a year the UVF was once again declared an illegal organization. When the UDA have contested seats they have met a similar fate, so that by the 1980s there were no more than a handful of elected representatives (from a total of over 500 councillors) with overt paramilitary connections.

Does that suggest that the protestant population is more law-abiding, more constitutionally minded, more politically committed than the catholic population? There is no overwhelming evidence to endorse this viewpoint. Its political leaders have proved well capable of what John Wilkes called 'playing the popular engines' by raising a mob and publicly fearing that they might lose control of it. The loyalist population has had a long tradition of indulging in the public procession (largely through annual Orange parades) as a political gesture. The bulk of these has passed off without incident but any history of Ulster from the mid-nineteenth century is replete with incidents of a sectarian nature. With the onset of the Troubles and growing fears for the legitimacy of the Stormont regime, loyalist leaders have indulged more and more in the politics of the street particularly if, like Ian Paisley, they did not possess a parliamentary platform. With the formation of the UDA several of these marches were headed by masked and becudgelled men full of threat and menace. While not publicly endorsed by the political leadership very few of these demonstrations were unequivocally condemned by them.

'Playing the popular engine', therefore, was one device whereby the paramilitaries might be embraced. After all, it could be claimed legitimately that groups like the UDA were 'counter-terrorist organizations' (to quote the UDA commander, Andy Tyrie) intent only on preserving the Ulster way of life. But if it looked as if these people might get out of control the politicians were ready to close ranks against a paramilitary takeover. The United Ulster Unionist Council (UUUC), formed to contest the February 1974 general election and composed of the anti-powersharing Ulster Unionist Party, the Democratic Unionists and Vanguard, really came into its own following the UWC victory in May. Concern that the paramilitaries might move more prominently into the political arena and control the agenda (as well as constituency seats) concentrated the mind wonderfully as the established politicians worked out a pact to conduct the Northern Ireland Convention election of May 1975. Having seen off the potential paramilitary challenge the parties returned to their internecine battles, and in May 1977 Official Unionist candidates stood in the local government elections without UUUC endorsement. By June it was accepted that the UUUC was dead but since the paramilitaries no longer presented an electoral threat its passing went largely unremarked.

A notable feature of the paramilitary role in the political sphere has been the UDA's capacity for original and progressive thought. Twice in the past decade when political dialogue has been sterile or nonexistent the UDA's 'think tank' has produced interesting documents. In March 1979 the New Ulster Political Research Group (NUPRG) published a set of constitutional ideas, 'Beyond The Religious Divide'. The document plumps for Ulster's independence as offering the best prospect for peace and stability. It suggests a constitution based on the US system of a separation of powers, a committee arrangement based on proportionality and a bill of rights. Its viability might be questioned but it was a genuine attempt to break the log jam.

More significantly, in the wake of the negative and destructive protests against the Anglo-Irish Agreement the NUPRG's successor, the Ulster Political Research Group, produced a remarkable document, 'Common Sense' (January 1987). The title itself is interesting because it is borrowed from the late eighteenth-century English republican, Thomas Paine, an unlikely source for Ulster loyalism. *Common Sense* explored questions of identity and displayed sensitivity towards minorities. It argued for an agreed process of government for Northern Ireland based on co-determination, on powersharing, on a bill of rights and a mutually agreed system for the administration of justice. It accepted the reality that the whole community was part of the process, that an exclusivist mentality was counter-productive and that the Agreement could serve as a catalyst.

Political parties representing protestant paramilitaries re-emerged as active players in the political scene following the IRA ceasefire of August 1994. When the loyalist cessation of violence was announced six weeks later, the 'Combined Loyalist Military Command' asserted that the decision had materially been influenced by the political arguments of the Progressive Unionist Party (PUP) and the Ulster Democratic Party (UDP). Neither the PUP, with a power base in the staunchly loyalist Shankill Road in west Belfast, nor the UDP, which had been formed in 1989 and had close links with the UDA, has had much electoral success. But as spokesmen for paramilitaries – analogues to Sinn Fein, they argue – both parties have together engaged in direct talks with British government officials, and they have displayed a measure of realism and flexibility which has sometimes been absent from the attitudes of the more mainstream unionist parties.

Since the beginning of the Troubles a bitter and divisive battle has gone on for control of the unionist leadership. We must remember that the Ulster Unionist Party had been the most successful political party in any liberal democracy since the 1920s. It had had absolute control of Northern Ireland until 1972. There had been the rare occasion when its dominance had been challenged by loyalist usurpers but all of them had been seen off the stage. Proportional representation for Stormont seats had been abolished before the third general election in 1929, for example, not because the party feared a nationalist revival but because it wanted to ensure that no other group could take on the mantle of defender of the constitution. In 1938 a Progressive Unionist Party contested twelve Stormont seats on a non-sectarian and radical economic programme but it failed to unseat any of the official candidates. Some working-class constituencies elected maverick candidates from time to time but virtually all of them were contained within the party straitjacket.

An exception to this rule was to be the Reverend Ian Paisley. He represented a fundamentalist strain in Irish protestantism which had been voluble since the rise of mass democracy. Whereas others have confined their roles largely to pressure-group activity he has been the first to direct a clear and sustained challenge on the unionist citadel through his own mass party organization – the Protestant Unionist Party which contested four local-government seats in Belfast in 1964 and in a bid to broaden its electoral appeal became the Democratic Unionist Party in 1971. It was the uncertainty concerning Northern Ireland's constitutional status and the perceived threat of a republican upsurge which brought him into politics. He personified and enlarged protestant fears in a period of great political uncertainty through simplistic and negative messages. He has had the great advantage that he has never served in government. As we shall see he and his party have been beneficiaries of fortuitous circumstances and he has grasped whatever opportunities, no matter how dubious, have come along.

Since the introduction of direct rule in 1972, Northern Ireland appears to have been in a perpetual state of electioneering. There have been six local council contests (1973, 1977, 1981, 1985, 1989 and 1993) and three Stormont-type elections: for the Northern Ireland Assembly in 1973 and again in 1982, and the Northern Ireland Constitutional Convention in 1975. In addition, general elections for the Westminster parliament were fought in February and October 1974, in 1979, 1983, 1987, 1992 and a series of fifteen by-elections on 23 January 1986 called as a result of the resignations of the sitting loyalist members protesting against the imposition of the Anglo-Irish Agreement. Finally, four elections have been held for the European Parliament. Two types of electoral system have been implemented: the British plurality system for Westminster elections; and the single-transferable-vote system of proportional representation for the rest. If nothing else the electorate has gained a certain sophistication and parties have acquired vital experience in fighting elections.

One of the first advantages which the recently founded DUP enjoyed was the introduction of proportional representation. Originally the electoral system was changed to encourage the growth of a nonsectarian middle ground. The creation of the biconfessional Alliance Party in 1970 was expected to fill this role but like other centre parties in Northern Ireland it has suffered from the fact that the middle ground is largely mythical. A secondary reason for the introduction of proportional representation was the destruction of the unionist monolith. In that it succeeded, as the results of the 1973 Assembly elections indicate. Where there had been one dominant Unionist Party up to and including 1969 (although then there had been pro- and anti-O'Neill factions) now there were no fewer than four unionist parties (and one independent loyalist) occupying fifty of the seventy-eight seats in the Assembly. Three of these parties, Vanguard with seven seats, DUP with eight and anti-White-Paper Unionists with eleven plus the independent candidate, occupied a solid bloc of seats united in their total rejection of the government's plan to establish a powersharing administration in Northern Ireland and to recognize that there was an Irish dimension whereby the government of the Republic had some role to play in the government of the North. In opposition to this bloc were the Faulkner Unionists who were committed to negotiating with other parties within the limits laid down in the White Paper. They believed themselves to be the heirs of the Ulster Unionist Party and held only twenty-three seats, a sad reflection on the divisions within the unionist 'family' exacerbated by the introduction of proportional representation.

So, the new electoral system had one desired result in that unionists had never been more visibly divided at any stage in their history. But it was won at the cost of enabling nascent parties propounding extremist views to find their place in the sun. The irony in all of this was that initially Ian Paisley had campaigned against the introduction of proportional representation since it was 'un-British'. He was to tell his tenth Annual Party Conference some years later that it was the providence of God which secured the introduction of proportional representation. A further consequence of this division was that it left the way open for someone or some party to exploit the divisions in unionism in an attempt to claim leadership of all unionists. Ian Paisley pursued this policy ruthlessly and in doing so saw off other pretenders to the crown. Although the DUP lags behind the Ulster Unionists in Westminster and local government elections, Paisley has consistently headed the poll in European votes. Thus the protestant community has been fairly evenly divided between the Ulster Unionists and Democratic Unionists. In the 1980s the intensity of this battle led to such acrimony and exaggerated pledges that a rational debate became impossible within the camp. As a result unionists tried to outbid each other in their claims to be the true loyalists. In turn this induced unrealistic expectations of what they might secure from the government in terms of their political future *and* it made them incapable of negotiating a meaningful compromise with their political opponents. None of this was to become apparent until the meaning of the Anglo-Irish Agreement was revealed.

Following the UWC strike in 1974 unionists had some reason to believe that collectively they were capable of exercising a veto on any government decision which was not to their liking. But its very success induced a sense of complacency and of rivalry among the various factions. The politician most connected with the strike was William Craig: Ian Paisley had absented himself from the first few days of the stoppage and was not wholly trusted by the strikers. The real strength of factionalism was revealed in the 1975 elections for a Northern Ireland Constitutional Convention, established by the government in an effort to stem loyalist paramilitary euphoria and to encourage the politicians to write their own constitution for a future Northern Ireland government. In the event Vanguard took two more seats than the DUP – fourteen and twelve respectively – with a smaller percentage of the vote, and the reconstituted Official Unionists, now led by Harry West, took nineteen seats.

The DUP was soon to recover the lost ground when William Craig made a fateful mistake in negotiations with the SDLP during the Convention. He suggested that there could be a powersharing government with the SDLP for the length of the emergency, in line with British political practice during the two World Wars. This was portrayed by other loyalists as a sign of appeasement, and the gesture split apart his own party. Craig never recovered.

Following the collapse of the Convention there were no further efforts made to resurrect devolved government until 1982. The battle within Unionism was now a two-horse race between the DUP and the UUP. Paisleyite tactics were based on a form of leadership destruction. One of his earliest slogans had been 'O'Neill must go'. It was to be followed at regular intervals by calls for the resignation of successive Unionist leaders – Chichester-Clark, Faulkner and West. All of them went in time but their departures could not be laid solely at the feet of Ian Paisley, much as he liked to claim the credit. The fact of the matter was that these individuals all represented an indigenous government which had allowed itself to be brought down by a combination of civil-rights cajolery and British wimpishness. They were easy targets to attack because they had to deal with the complex problems of actual government or the assumed leadership of the unionist people. If there had to be scapegoats they were the most easily identified as such. Besides the Ulster Unionist Party had undergone a genuine trauma. Out of office for the first time since 1920, rudderless and uncertain of which way to jump they seemed to lack both principle and moral fibre. Paisleyism offered certainty.

One fundamental question for *all* unionists since the imposition of direct rule was their meaning of unionism and how it should manifest itself. The debate broke down roughly into three camps – those who favoured an independent state, those who wanted devolution and those who desired integration into the British system in a manner akin to Scotland and Wales. The first option has never been too popular if only because the economics of independence was too bleak to contemplate. It remains a fallback position to be considered only in a dire emergency. As direct rule became more permanent and the British government laid out the lines of its policy devolutionists became conscious of the fact that there would never be a return to the old Stormont system. Their internal debate has centred on the degree of power and responsibility they are prepared to concede to the minority. The 'debate', it needs to be said, has been conducted *sotto voce* and with no great enthusiasm but it has the merit of displaying a modicum of realism. The integrationists have evaded this despotism of fact since in their United Kingdom there is no need for devolved structures, and hence no need to share power. They seem oblivious to the fact that opinion polls from Britain suggest that very few indeed of the British electorate welcome closer links with Northern Ireland. Similarly MPs have not been noted for their rush to promote the integrationist case. Instead integrationists have reverted to a hazy nostalgia and have adopted Sir Edward Carson as their mentor. Devolution, they assert, was a device foistered on the province by Britain which unionists in 1920 did not seek. There is some historic merit in this argument but it ignores the fact that by the mid-1920s, when unionists saw the benefit of controlling their own destiny virtually free of Westminster's interference, they became enthusiastic devolutionists. A 1936 report of the Ulster Unionist Council sums up this attitude: 'Northern Ireland without a Parliament of her own would be a standing temptation to certain British Politicians to make another bid for a final settlement with the Irish Republic.'

In the absence of any proper surveillance from Westminster and the lack of any critical unionist opposition these questions could be set aside. All of that changed, of course, with direct rule and it was the flagship of unionism, the Ulster Unionist Party, which had to carry the brunt of the debate. This was to have relevance to the intra-unionist battle since it gave the DUP another weapon to undermine UUP morale. We have seen that the DUP had certain advantages. Since it had not been in government – nor even in existence – then it could not be held responsible for the civil rights debacle. Nor had it spawned the 'traitor' O'Neill and his weak-kneed successors. Indeed one of the striking differences in the two parties was the nature and security of the leadership. The Ulster Unionist Party had from its inception been a 'bottom up' party – that is, its leaders had to keep in close touch with grassroots opinion. After all it was the Orange lodges with their fraternal instincts which had launched and sustained the party; and it was devolution and a highly decentralized local-government structure which added to the sense of importance of the individual activist. The DUP, on the other hand, was very much the property of its leader, Ian Paisley. His undoubted rhetorical and organizational gifts gave him total command over the rank and file. When he spoke the party spoke.

The UUP had a second problem. It had always had very strong Westminster representation so that in the absence of devolved institutions for most of the period after 1972 its MPs saw Westminster as the real seat of power. They had some reason to do so. They enjoyed very good relations with the Conservative Party and had taken the party whip for decades. By the late 1970s the imposition of direct rule and the Ted Heath interregnum were seen as hiccups which had been overcome satisfactorily. Since the October 1974 general election Unionists probably had a much higher profile in the Commons than other regional parties because from then on they had an MP, Enoch Powell, who was an outstanding parliamentarian. In addition, they held a pivotal position of a bloc of ten votes in a parliament in which the Labour government was struggling to hold on to a majority. The unionist bloc was able to trade these seats in return for a promise that Northern Ireland's representation at Westminster would be increased to seventeen seats (a promise delivered in time for the 1983 general election). Here were the palpable signs of political clout. Further, the Conservative spokesman on Northern Ireland from 1975, Airey Neave, was a convinced integrationist who had the ear of the new Tory leader, Margaret Thatcher. He had a plan to restore some of the lost powers of local government in the province and to integrate the system more fully

into the British. In these circumstances integrationism became
popular with the unionist leadership. Many of the secondary
leadership, however, those who would aspire to a seat in a
devolved institution, found no outlet for their talents beyond
the small pond of local government. There was, too, a political
objection to integration. It was the Commons and the government
which had signed the Sunningdale agreement and which was later
to be party to the Anglo-Irish Agreement. How could a small bloc
of provincial MPs overturn the might of Westminster? It was
precisely this worry which enabled Ian Paisley persuade his own
party to engage wholeheartedly in the Northern Ireland Assembly
created by James Prior. It would, he said, be 'a bulwark for the
Union'; it would give the unionist family another platform with
which to negotiate with the British. As a corollary, it would
emphasize the distinctiveness of 'Ulster', a concept which was
gaining greater popularity as more loyalists came to mistrust the
British. In that sense the devolutionists could embrace those who
favoured independence.

It is against this background that we examine the contest
between the DUP and the UUP. The Northern Ireland
Constitutional Convention was formally dissolved by Westminster
Order on 9 March 1976. It was to be more than six years before
another attempt at devolution was made. At that time the DUP
had one paid political representative, Ian Paisley, MP for Antrim
North. The party had won twenty-one out of the 526 seats at
the 1973 local council elections and appeared as little more than
a minor irritant on the unionist periphery. Yet by 1979 they held
three Westminster seats and were the second most powerful
grouping in unionist-controlled local councils with seventy-four
seats and 12.7 per cent of the vote. More significantly, Ian Paisley
had inflicted a very damaging blow to the UUP leadership when he
topped the poll in the direct elections to the European Parliament
with a massive 170,688 first preference votes, almost 30 per
cent of the total. It enabled him to proclaim that he was the
most popular loyalist leader ever and that his victory had been
engineered by the mysterious providence of God. No longer

could he be ignored or patronized by respectable unionists. He
had reached the high ground and would make the running. He
had been making the running before this, of course. He had led
the 1977 'constitutional stoppage' with the overt support of the
paramilitary UDA who wished to persuade the authorities to go
on the offensive against the IRA and to restore Stormont. He
undertook this adventure without the backing of the mainstream
unionist parties and the rift between them led to the disbanding
of the UUUC. It also contributed to deep personal animosity
between Paisley and Powell, who later was to describe Paisley
as 'the most resourceful, inveterate and dangerous enemy of the
Union'. And yet we have seen that one month later, in the first
real free-for-all contest between the unionist parties at the local
council elections, the DUP did remarkably well. Steve Bruce, a
relatively sympathetic academic observer of Paisleyism, explains it
thus: 'because he was still *ideologically sound*, strategic and tactical
mistakes could be forgiven' (*God Save Ulster! The Religion and
Politics of Paisleyism*, Oxford, 1986, p. 115).

Again, in the aftermath of the Provisionals' assassination of
the Reverend Robert Bradford, UUP MP for Belfast South,
and of the burgeoning Anglo-Irish process, Paisley established a
'Third Force' ostensibly to complement the official security effort.
Later his party was connected with Ulster Resistance, a shadowy
organization opposed to the Hillsborough Agreement. None of this
activity seemed to damage the electoral prospects of his party, and
in the 1984 European election he increased his personal vote to
33.6 per cent. But it may be that the DUP vote had peaked, as
the statistics in table 4.1 reveal. These figures must be handled
with some caution. In the first place the European election
results demonstrate, as noted above, the personal dominance
of Ian Paisley, notably his exceptional performance in 1984.
At the local government level the DUP have subsided from
the mid-1980s return, which approached a quarter of the vote,
to a plateau of 17-odd per cent. In the Westminster contests,
agreements between the two unionist parties not to split the
unionist vote have affected the results. This has to be borne

Table 4.1 UUP and DUP electoral statistics (as percentages) 1982–1994

	1982 (Assembly)	1983 (Westminster)	1984 (Europe)	1985 (Local government)	1987 (Westminster)
UUP	29.7	34.0	21.5	29.5	37.8
DUP	23.0	20.0	33.6	24.3	11.7

	1989 (Local government)	1989 (Europe)	1992 (Westminster)	1993 (Local government)	1994 (Europe)
UUP	31.3	22.2	34.5	29.4	23.8
DUP	17.7	29.9	13.1	17.3	29.2

in mind when comparing 1983 and 1987. Here the DUP vote
fell by more than 8 per cent, whereas the UUP rose by 4 per
cent. It may be argued that the DUP lost no seats (they have
won three Westminster seats in each of the general elections
from 1983 to 1992), but the following important fact needs to
be borne in mind: in 1983 DUP candidates had run a number
of UUP candidates a very close second and hence they looked
forward to challenging them in 1987. But the two party leaders,
Ian Paisley and James Molyneaux, had agreed an electoral pact
that there was to be a united loyalist front against the Anglo-Irish
Agreement, and so no sitting MPs were to be challenged. This
proved to be a major concession to the UUP who could easily
have lost two seats to the DUP and with them a further drain on
party morale. In the circumstances it was the DUP morale which
suffered and a number of their more promising younger members
deserted the party. Although the DUP staged a modest recovery
in 1992, its political clout continues to depend disproportionately
on the person of its leader.

This leads to one final comment. The DUP tactic of demanding
the resignation of one unionist leader after another seems to have
ground to a halt largely because the incumbent since 1979, James
Molyneaux, has proved too wily for Ian Paisley. Molyneaux seems
to be the antithesis of Paisley, colourless and lacklustre, but he
has displayed considerable talent in holding his fissiparous party
together at a period when it was split on tactics, on ideology
and on personality. Molyneaux simply let the DUP make all the
running whether at the parapolitical or extra-parliamentary level.
Molyneaux's position was strengthened by the close relationship
which developed between him and the British prime minister, John
Major, especially after the April 1992 Westminster general election
which left the Conservative government with a significantly reduced
majority and therefore grateful for the support of the nine Ulster
Unionist MPs. Molyneaux accepted Major's assurances after the
Joint Declaration and the publication of the Framework documents
that 'the Union was safe', yet by 1995 UUP concerns about the
direction of the peace process and jockeying for position in the

anticipated leadership context (Molyneaux was born in August 1920) had begun to undermine the unionist leader's position. Over fifteen years, nevertheless, he had preserved the unity of his party, but the price that he paid may have been an inability to read the political landscape correctly and to be in a position to negotiate from strength. It is as if the unionist parties engaged in their own form of frenzied dialogue and thereby lost a sense of perspective.

This chapter has concentrated on a discrete contest inside one community. Missing from the political equation has been what are called middle-ground parties. Among these is the Alliance Party, effectively a unionist body, which holds that the constitutional status quo should only be altered by consent within Northern Ireland. It is the only major party in the province which draws significant support from both sides of the community. Yet it has never been able successfully to challenge the dominance of the leading unionist and nationalist parties. We have noted that proportional representation was introduced to expand the mythical centre, but it has continued to remain mythical. Edward Moxon-Browne's portrait of the Alliance Party as being middle-aged, Belfast-centred, non-manual and possessing a higher proportion of higher educated than the other parties may explain why it was not successful. It did not seem to relate to the emotions of the combatants, and it was this self-conscious thrust towards reasons and reasonableness which may have made it redundant.

In that respect Alliance was not much different from earlier 'centre' parties, like the Ulster Liberals and the Northern Ireland Labour Party (NILP). The latter held four of the fifty-two Stormont seats in the early 1960s but was swept aside in the emotion engendered by the civil rights movement. Alliance has suffered a similar fate. When inter-communal tensions rise Alliance support dips. It took 9.2 per cent of the vote in the 1973 Assembly elections and played a useful role in the powersharing executive. But while it could hope to muster about 10 per cent of the vote in the 1970s, this proportion dropped in the 1980s and 90s. In the 1989 local government elections the party won a 6.8 per cent vote, which improved to 7.6 per cent in 1993. The party seems destined to be no more than a small liberal ginger-group. Its best hope lies in a devolved system when it can expect to raise its visibility as it did with its ten members in the Assembly which met in 1982.

5 Nationalist Politics

After the establishment of Northern Ireland in 1921, catholics – the minority – were largely excluded from politics in the new polity. The slow development of active nationalist political representation, moreover, was inevitably influenced by the prevailing unionist domination of the province and the extent to which unionists themselves actually set the political agenda. Nationalist participation in the Northern Ireland political system was further constrained by two other factors. First was the feeling that such involvement would tend to legitimize the unionist 'statelet' and so entrench partition. Second was the widely-held assumption that partition was only a temporary phenomenon and that Northern Ireland itself could not survive for very long as a separate political entity. Nationalists, however, underestimated both the increasing unionist commitment to Northern Ireland on a long-term basis and Britain's extreme reluctance to get involved any further with Ireland. Most importantly, perhaps, nationalists in both the North and the South failed to appreciate the need, if partition were to be minimized, to conciliate and accommodate the unionists in any future Irish political arrangements – in short the need to take unionism seriously as a legitimate political position for people living on the island of Ireland.

The failure of constitutional nationalists within Northern Ireland (as had been the case with their Redmondite predecessors) to face up creatively to the challenge posed by the unionists – not, of course that the latter gave them much encouragement – allowed physical force nationalists to make much of the political running. Republicans sporadically launched violent attacks in Northern Ireland (and Great Britain) in the 1930s and 1940s. A co-ordinated campaign concentrated along the border was mounted by the IRA between 1956 and 1962 and claimed the lives of six policemen and eleven republican activists or sympathizers. That it was not more successful had much to do with its own incompetence and its failure to garner enough covert sympathy from the catholic minority, above all in Belfast. In the absence of any sustained nationalist engagement in the Northern Ireland political process, the violent threat to the province's very existence dominated unionist perceptions of nationalist politics.

Even when an (initially) non-violent challenge was mounted to unionist policies, the regime – with deplorable consequences – largely took it to be no more than a further manifestation of the long-standing republican campaign to destroy Northern Ireland. With dreadful irony, in a kind of self-fulfilling prophesy, the Belfast government's own responses to the nationalist-dominated civil rights agitation helped to transform what had essentially been a campaign to reform the internal affairs of Northern Ireland into a violent situation which threatened to bring down the whole political structure of the province as it had existed since 1921.

Spearheading the armed challenge to the Northern Ireland *status quo* over twenty-five years has been the Provisional IRA which self-consciously embodies a sense of continuity with Ireland's ancient martyrs. It is a commonplace that the Irish are too interested in history and that they invoke the ghosts of history to justify present actions. Hence in its very first public statement the Provisional Army Council (formed in January 1970) declared its allegiance to 'the 32 county Irish Republic *proclaimed at Easter 1916* established by the First Dail Eireann in 1919, over-thrown by force of arms in 1922 and suppressed to this day by the existing British-imposed six county and twenty-six county partition states'. The hunger strikes of 1980 and 1981 compounded this capacity to draw on symbols which reinforced the Provisionals' claim to be the authentic republicans to such an extent that Christ was invoked: 'No greater love hath a man than to lay down his life for his friends'. A similar thrust can be found in loyalist circles. In a distinguished history of loyalism, *Queen's Rebels*, David Miller traces a tradition of 'public banding', whereby the protestant people of Ulster relied on their own resources to defend themselves, from the seventeenth century up to and including the formation of the Ulster Volunteer Force (UVF) to resist the Third Home Rule Bill of 1912, and the 'B Specials' which were in existence from 1920 to 1969. If the Ulster Covenant of 1912 (a solemn declaration committing Ulster to the Union and loyalty to the Crown, signed by 471,414 persons) symbolizes the determination and aspirations of the loyalist people, then the 1916 Proclamation with its declaration of an Irish Republic fulfils the same role for republicans. Both of them use the same ominous phrase – 'all means necessary' – to delineate the lengths to which they are prepared to go.

In times of crisis (and Northern Ireland has never enjoyed a sustained period of normality) there is a tendency to resurrect ancestral heroes, who may provide overt support to each community's paramilitaries. Thus, in the period of great uncertainty following the signing of the Anglo-Irish Agreement, many protestants recalled the memories of Sir Edward Carson and Sir James Craig, the architects of Northern Ireland, and some have tried to emulate the organization of the original UVF. Similarly, the Provisionals have drawn on a republican heritage reaching back to Wolfe Tone in the late eighteenth century and since 1970 they have been able to masquerade as the protectors of the catholic minority. As elections statistics will show, moreover, their political wing, Sinn Fein, has converted this into some political clout.

This needs some explanation before we embark on an examination of electoral fortunes in the 1970s. It is not that the people of Northern Ireland are particularly amoral, although propogandists on both sides attempt to portray their adversaries in lurid terms. Rather than attempting a detailed analysis of the reasons for community support for paramilitaries, we shall refer briefly to the position of the Provisional movement. Already we have observed one reason for its tenacity – continuity. A group which can demonstrate lineage with ancient heroes starts with certain advantages, but these cannot be sustained unless that community perceives a threat to its values if not to its very existence.

The political environment in which the Provisionals operate offers another explanation. One reason given for embarking on the hunger strike which was to claim ten prisoners' lives in 1981 was 'to advance the Irish people's right for liberty'. This demand strikes a highly-tuned emotional chord among a section of the population which believes that partition of the island in 1921 was immoral and was achieved solely through the loyalist threat of violence. The only proper response was to reply in kind. In that respect the genesis of Provisionalism is interesting. The Provisional IRA was formed after the 'old' Official IRA split in December 1969. It draws its title from the proclamation of the provisional government of the Republic of Ireland at the start of the Easter Rising in 1916, and affirms that any government in Ireland will be 'provisional' until the final establishment of a thirty-two county republic. Believing in the ultimate unity of the people of Ireland and the essential geographical and political indivisibility of the island, its primary immediate objective is to secure the withdrawal (as republicans see it) of British forces from Northern Ireland. It was not simply another manifestation of armed republicanism. It was born following loyalist attacks on the catholic ghettoes of west Belfast in August 1969. Its personnel were the young people of those areas intent on defending themselves. The graffito of the time – 'IRA = I Ran Away' – captures the sense of despair felt by many residents who believed that the old IRA leadership was more intent on conducting seminars in Marxist theory rather than looking after their own. The new breed were more indigenous and more ruthless. They were the children of the ghetto and until the mid-1970s when the IRA reverted to a cellular system they were organized on a neighbourhood basis.

Much of the Provisionals' success depended upon military and security insensitivity. Between 1971 and 1978 inclusive there were more than 300,000 house searches, most of which would have occurred in republican areas. Not all of these, by any means, would have been conducted sensitively, and they were widely viewed as forms of community assault. The political response to the Provisionals, moreover, was inconsistent. The dualism of British government policy towards the organization is well illustrated by the events of 1972. After the establishment of direct rule in March, it seemed that perhaps after all London might consider a major change in the province's constitutional status. The introduction in June of 'special category' status – effectively a political status for convicted terrorists – was correctly taken by the Provisionals as a sign that the British government might be prepared to parley with them, even against the advice of the government of the Republic. On 26 June the Provisionals called a ceasefire. Early in July secret talks were held in Paul Channon's house in London between the Secretary of State for Northern Ireland, William Whitelaw, and representatives of the Provisional leadership, including Sean MacStiofain, the Chief of Staff, Martin McGuinness from Derry and Gerry Adams, who had been released from detention especially for the occasion. The talks came to nothing and the ceasefire was called off soon afterwards. The Provisionals presented to Whitelaw a list of fixed demands, which they apparently thought the Cabinet might consider. Among these was that the British government should declare its intention 'to withdraw all British forces from Irish soil' before the beginning of 1975. Whether the Provisionals' delegation really believed that the British might accede to their wishes, or whether the whole affair was no more than a propaganda exercise on their part, these absolutely fixed demands disabused Whitelaw and his colleagues of any pious hopes they may have had that they could negotiate as politicians with the Provisional leadership.

Until 1995 the government avoided any similar direct high-level links with illegal paramilitary groups, although from time to time some secret contacts were made. After 1972 it was hoped that the political wing of the movement – Provisional Sinn Fein (PSF) – which was legalized in 1974 might in some way be encouraged to wean republican activists away from violence. During another Provisional ceasefire in the spring of 1975 joint 'incident centres' were set up, manned by government officials and members of PSF. This ceasefire also collapsed with the British government's refusal to accept the Provisionals' *sine qua non* – the demand for 'Brits out'. With the success of PSF candidates in local council elections in the 1980s, and the election in 1983 of Gerry Adams as Westminster member for West Belfast, the Provisional leadership maintained the so-called 'ballot paper in one hand and Armalite rifle in the other' strategy. This was not without strains. At the Provisional Sinn Fein annual conference in November 1986 a group styling itself 'Republican Sinn Fein' broke away from the main organization after the conference had voted to take up any seats its candidates might win in the Dublin parliament.

Loyalist activity (and rhetoric) has contributed to republican success. The New Ireland Forum calculated that in the period from 1969 to mid-1983 loyalist paramilitary groups were responsible for 613 deaths. Of course they had also been involved in the UWC strike of 1974, the constitutional stoppage of 1977, the creation of the 'Third Force' in 1981, and of the Ulster Clubs movement in 1985. The relative political success which the republican movement seemed to enjoy in the early 1990s contributed to a revival of loyalist sectarian killings and attacks on republican activists. In short, paramilitaries feed off each other and their respective communities remain reluctant to abandon them to a (British) government whose credentials are dubious.

An examination of the genesis of loyalist paramilitarism would reveal the same pattern, although its ledger of violence is not of the same magnitude and its self-perception as a counter-terrorist organization has had some validity. However, the nationalist retort that the security forces had traditionally looked after the interests of the protestant community underlines the complexity of the problem and the difficulties in pursuing a solely political path.

Suffice it to say that community ambivalence towards political violence is grounded in constitutional uncertainty, genuine communal fears and a history of unstability. All of that must be appreciated before one tries to understand why the political process has faltered.

When Danny Morrison, Sinn Fein Director of Publicity, asserted at the 1981 conference that republicans had 'a ballot paper in one hand and an Armalite rife in the other' he was reflecting the euphoria of an organization which believed that it had ceased to be a sect and had become a mass movement. A year later the same sentiment appeared in the Sinn Fein newspaper *An Phoblacht* in the run up to the Northern Ireland Assembly elections. 'The essence of republican struggle', it declared, 'must be in armed resistance coupled with popular opposition to the British presence. So, while not everyone can plant a bomb, everyone can plant a vote'. This displayed a cynicism based on the arrogance of a movement which believed that its time had come. It had some reason to support this belief, but such was the apprehension aroused by the Provisionals that the mainstream political parties set out to remove whatever ambivalence to violence existed in the community. That task fell largely on the SDLP.

Until the hunger strikes the SDLP had enjoyed a virtually unchallenged political position within the catholic community. There were several reasons for this. The most obvious was that there was no competition. With the passing exception of the Irish Independence Party, formed in 1977 on the more militant policy of seeking British withdrawal, the SDLP had a clear run. The IIP secured 3.3 per cent of the vote in the 1979 general election and 3.9 per cent in the 1981 local government elections but faded thereafter when its vote swung over to Sinn Fein.

Secondly we need to look at the nature of the SDLP. It has been the most successful party to represent the minority since partition. Until its appearance, the opposition was noted for its lack of organization. Its chief flagship, the Nationalist Party, had contested elections without a party headquarters and without paid officials. Until November 1964 it did not even have a party programme, save the principle of dismantling Northern Ireland as a political entity in favour of Irish unity. The SDLP, on the other hand, was formed on the enthusiasm whipped up by civil rights victories with the ensuing unionist discomfort. It was formed, too, with a distinct ideology and a strong belief in organization. In the Northern Irish context two of the party's objectives were noteworthy: 'to organise and maintain in Northern Ireland a Socialist Party', and 'to promote the cause of Irish unity based on the consent of the majority of people in Northern Ireland'. The first of these was realized through its membership of the Socialist International and the Confederation of Socialist Parties of the European Community. But the political terrain in which it worked and the fundamental problems which it encountered made the SDLP an atypical member of the European Socialist movement and its socialist credentials are more cosmetic than real.

It was atypical in the Northern nationalist tradition as well in that it accepted the doctrine of consent if Irish unity was to be realized. Unlike the old Nationalist Party it had to cast its appeal well beyond the narrow confines of a permanent catholic minority, and that meant paying attention to such things as organization and electoral appeal. Rather than be a single-issue party, it had to become a 'catch-more' party. It could not expect to be a 'catch-all' party in that it appreciated that its ideology was antithetical to traditional unionists. Rather, it had to woo waverers. Unlike Sinn Fein it did not believe in the armed struggle, and it had to offer a programme of hope which would remove the minority from despair and the clutches of the gunmen.

We shall see from the voting figures that the SDLP has had mixed success in these objects, but that the quality of tenacity is one which has remained with it through adversity. Paradoxically, the party may have benefited from lack of electoral success. With the exception of the short period January–May 1974, when it was in office as part of the powersharing administration, and some success in the largely powerless arena of local government, it has been consigned to a political limbo. Its republican opponents have been able to proclaim that this demonstrates that the minority cannot expect fair play inside the 'gerrymandered statelet' and that Northern Ireland is irreformable. If the SDLP continues – or so the propaganda would have it – it is because its members are unprincipled and are prepared to sell their nationalist souls for a mess of partitionist, powersharing pottage. To remain in the business of influencing the political debate, therefore, the SDLP has had to change its tactics to meet the twin challenges posed by the adversity of the internal electoral system and the seductive simplicity of 'the Armalite rifle and the ballot box'.

All of this has had an energizing effect on the party. The engineered collapse of the powersharing executive in 1974 and the subsequent refusal of the unionist parties to contemplate any form of powersharing acceptable to the British government has induced the SDLP to alter its strategy to include an enhanced role for Dublin in the political process. One tangible success of this strategy is to be seen in the Anglo-Irish Agreement with its tacit 'internationalization' of the Northern Ireland problem and its short-term neutralization of the unionist veto. The architect of the new policy, John Hume (leader of the party since 1979) spelt it out in 1979 in an article for the prestigious American journal *Foreign Affairs* when he asserted that London and Dublin would have to act together in 'a positive and decisive initiative' which would remove any 'unconditional guarantees for any section of the northern community', and that the whole community must be made to realize that there are no simple solutions but only a process that will lead to a solution. In other words he was asserting the primacy of the political and the fundamental responsibilities of the two sovereign states.

This strategy unfolded through the Anglo-Irish process, beginning with a summit meeting in May 1980 and including other developments such as the report on the situation in Northern Ireland drawn up on behalf of the Political Affairs Committee of the European Parliament by Neils Haagerup and tabled on 2 March 1984. In the domestic domain the strategy enabled the party to keep its head above water as it came under increasing electoral pressure from Sinn Fein and equal pressure from the then Secretary of State, James Prior, who was intent on making one last move towards a purely internal settlement when he created his Northern Ireland Assembly in October 1982. The SDLP fought that election on a policy of boycotting the Assembly, a policy incidentally also espoused by Sinn Fein. In fact Sinn Fein accused the SDLP of adopting the boycott tactic simply because they would suffer the wrath of the minority community if they had done anything different.

The SDLP response was the establishment of the New Ireland Forum with the task of redefining Irish nationalism in the light of contemporary events and attitudes. Its membership was drawn from the SDLP and the three major constitutional parties in the Republic – Fianna Fail, Fine Gael and Labour. In that respect its proponents could claim that it spoke for the vast majority of the Irish population. The Forum met for an eleven-month period in competition with the Northern Ireland Assembly and published its final report on 2 May 1984. The report did not meet universal approbation simply because it was an Irish nationalist report which expressed the age-old desire for Irish unity. In addition it suggested variants of that theme in models of federalism / confederalism and of joint Irish / British authority over Northern Ireland. The report stressed that unity could only be achieved 'in agreement' and it also provided itself with a failsafe mechanism in paragraph 5.10 when it declared its willingness 'to discuss other views which may contribute to political development'.

The New Ireland Forum helped to set the Northern Ireland political agenda by putting the onus on the British government to respond positively. In a Commons debate on 2 July 1984 John Hume stated: 'The most important aspect of the report is not the three options, but the views of Irish Nationalists about the ways in which realities must be faced if there is to be a solution.' If nothing else, the Forum exercise was a brilliant piece of public relations which commanded international attention, made much of the effort of the Assembly appear redundant, ensured that the SDLP continued to hog the limelight, and, as a corollary, halted the onward march on Sinn Fein. The latter is clear from the electoral statistics in table 5.1. Sinn Fein are far from being a spent force but the above suggests that where the SDLP can dictate the agenda then the republican drive loses much of its momentum. A closer examination of the figures in the context of recent events reveals that the SDLP are continuing to battle inside the nationalist community. Sinn Fein have been unable to capture more than about a third of the entire nationalist vote, and peaked with just over 13 per cent of the total poll in the mid-1980s. Gerry Adams' election as Westminster MP for West Belfast in 1983, and his re-election in 1987, was an important demonstration of Sinn Fein strength and a powerful boost for Adams' own kudos. Conversely the loss of the seat in 1992 to the SDLP, whose candidate evidently attracted some protestant votes, was a significant blow. Sinn Fein have been most successful at local-government level where it is now the fourth largest party in the province. In Belfast in 1993 it won more votes than any other single party, outpolling the SDLP in West Belfast. Sinn Fein also competes in elections in the Republic, and two hunger-strikers won seats in 1982. But this success has not been repeated and the party has never gained more than 2 per cent of the vote.

If the SDLP's control of the agenda was one explanation for Sinn Fein's slippage, another reason lay in the activities of the IRA. A high public profile has meant that Sinn Fein spokesmen were frequently called upon to justify republican violence. Adams in particular calmly and articulately rationalized and defended attacks, however brutal and publicly identified himself with the IRA, such as when he helped to carry the coffin of bomber Thomas Begley who blew himself up in the Shankill bombing of October 1993. But this demeanour did not always square in the public mind with what is commonly understood as the democratic process. One of the most damaging reports of the New Ireland Forum exercise, for example, was entitled 'The Cost of Violence arising from the Northern Ireland Crisis since 1969'. It illustrated graphically the damage done to minority communities by the IRA

Table 5.1 Sinn Fein and Social Democratic and Labour Party electoral statistics (as percentages) 1982–1994

	1982 (Assembly)	1983 (Westminster)	1984 (Europe)	1985 (Local government)	1987 (Westminster)
SF	10.1	13.4	13.3	11.8	11.4
SDLP	18.8	17.9	22.1	17.8	21.1

	1989 (Local government)	1989 (Europe)	1992 (Westminster)	1993 (Local government)	1994 (Europe)
SF	11.2	9.1	10.0	12.4	9.0
SDLP	21.0	25.5	23.5	22.0	28.9

in terms of fatal incidents and industrial- and commercial-sector damage done in selected towns.

But, as will be noted in chapter 8, Adams has also shifted the Sinn Fein debate increasingly towards a more political (as opposed to military) strategy. This, too, was reinforced by John Hume's willingness to engage Adams in talks, initially in 1988 and again in 1993. For many unionists the Sinn Fein–SDLP contacts appeared to represent the emergence of a 'pan-nationalist front', apparently dedicated to the securing of traditional nationalist objectives. But the two parties remain competitors for the votes of the Northern Ireland minority, and it remains to be seen whether a longer-term effect of the republican cessation of violence in August 1994 will be to enhance Sinn Fein's electoral fortunes.

It may seem that we have spent too much time in the chapters on nationalist and unionist politics fishing around the extremes. The fact of the matter, as Richard Rose explained in 1976, is that Northern Ireland's party system is different from that in any other western nation: 'It more nearly resembles the party system of a Latin American country, where military and foreign involvement in politics are taken for granted, or that of Weimar Germany or the First Austrian Republic between the wars when armed groups competed with parties for the power to rule' (*Northern Ireland: A Time of Choice*, Macmillan, 1976, p. 69). Northern Ireland is not quite as stark as that, but there can be little question that the party system and its relationship to paramilitarism reflects the harsh and unstable political environment in which it operates.

6 Keeping the Peace

At its most simplistic level, and at the level of many popular British perceptions, the chief security challenge in Northern Ireland for most of the period from 1969 to 1994 was posed by the 250 or so serving volunteers – gunmen, bombers and so on – of the Provisional IRA. It follows, therefore, that all the security forces had to do to 'solve' the Northern Ireland problem was to eliminate these volunteers. But the challenge was and is, in reality, much more complex. Although the Provisionals constituted the single most important terrorist organization in the province, they are as much a symptom of 'the Troubles' as a cause. We have already noted the significance of violence in Irish, and Northern Irish, political culture. The Provisionals, together with other republican and loyalist paramilitary groups, express the pragmatic and continuing faith which some political activists in the island retain in the usefulness of violent methods. In the past, violence, actual or threatened, has been effective for both republicans and loyalists.

Whatever happens in the political sphere, 'hard core' paramilitaries may very well retain this romantic faith for ever and continue to present, if residually, a classic 'military' or terrorist challenge to the security forces, which in turn will stimulate a straightforward police / military response. But equally important in any security effort is the need to provide effective – and therefore broadly accepted – constitutional mechanisms for the expression of legitimate political aspirations. Any response to a challenge which is in fact both violent and political must also reflect this duality.

The three main republican paramilitary groups – the Official IRA, the Irish National Liberation Army and the Provisional IRA – illustrate the complexities of the security challenge from the nationalist side. By the late 1960s the old IRA, which after the formation of the Provisionals became known as the Official IRA, had largely abandoned its commitment to an armed struggle in favour of a Marxist political strategy promoted by the chief of staff, Cathal Goulding. Although after 1969 it embarked on a violent campaign against the army and the RUC, in May 1972 the organization declared a unilateral ceasefire, asserting that continued violence was an impediment to the development of working-class solidarity. The political wing of the Officials subsequently developed into the Workers' Party, which gained representation in the Dublin parliament. It has also conducted high-profile political campaigns in the North, although it has consistently failed to attract much electoral support especially sine the party was seriously weakened by a split in 1992 over continued paramilitary links, and a new group, the Democratic Left, broke away. Since 1972 the Official IRA seems largely to have fallen into abeyance and it does not currently pose any direct security threat. In recent years, nevertheless, assertions have been made that the organization continues to be involved in armed robberies and protection rackets of various types.

The Irish National Liberation Army (INLA) was established in December 1974 by members of the Officials who opposed the Goulding-inspired ceasefire. The following year it also gained recruits from the Provisionals, such as Dominic McGlinchey, who were disenchanted by the Provisionals' spring ceasefire. The INLA developed as perhaps the most uncompromising and ruthless of the Northern Irish terrorist organizations, adopting a strict anti-British, anti-protestant and apparently Marxist military strategy. Despite the existence of a political wing, the Irish Republican Socialist Party, the INLA's emphasis was on a purely military strategy and a policy of extreme terror, especially in border areas such as south Armagh, where they attacked a pentecostalist service at Darkley in November 1983, killing three worshippers and injuring seven. The INLA was never very large – police estimates put its maximum numbers at fewer than one hundred – and it suffered seriously from informers in the early 1980s. Its operations were disrupted by a serious internal feud which broke out at the end of 1986 and led to a series of killings on both sides of the border. The organization has only intermittently surfaced since then.

Over the past twenty-five years the Provisionals became perhaps the most sophisticated and experienced terrorist group in western Europe. They began, however, as more of a vigilante force, organized to defend – as the Official IRA had evidently failed to do – the catholic community from attack by extreme protestant mobs. They were also prepared to take advantage of the fluid and unstable conditions produced by the civil rights agitation and the Stormont government's clumsy handling of it. Although British troops were at first cautiously welcomed in catholic areas when they were initially deployed in 1969 (and, indeed, the army co-operated with known IRA leaders to keep the peace in west Belfast), when it emerged that London's policy was designed merely to reform the existing political system in Northern Ireland, rather than to sweep it away in anticipation of a united Ireland, the IRA moved on to the offensive against the British Army.

On the military side the Provisionals pursued three main lines of attack. At the beginning their role as protectors of the catholic community soon developed into one of mobilizing the community into mass demonstrations, both violent and peaceful. Large-scale street disorder – in both protestant and catholic parts of Belfast and Derry – was characteristic of the early days of the Troubles. Although for the most part these riots were not 'organized' in any systematic sense, paramilitaries from both sides certainly sought to capitalize on the disorder and opportunistically use it to promote their own ends. An outbreak of street violence, for example, might draw security-force personnel into a locality where they could be attacked by bombers or snipers. In a more general fashion the encouragement of disorder in the hope that the security forces might overreact might itself serve to radicalize the local community and in turn enhance the paramilitaries' role as protectors. In recent years, however, the incidence of widespread street unrest has dropped considerably. Even the annual demonstrations commemorating particularly sensitive anniversaries, such as that of internment on 9 August or Bloody Sunday on 30 January, are now generally marked only by sporadic street violence. With the development of a strong political side to their activity, indeed, the Provisionals have even felt it to be in their best interests to keep mass demonstrations peaceful. Riots themselves, after all, can damage and unsettle the very communities where the Provisionals seek to consolidate their support. During the 1981 hunger strikes, for example, quite broadly-based popular support was mobilized in peaceful public demonstrations behind the strikers by a 'National H-Block Committee', which comprised a broad spectrum of republican opinion, not just those sympathetic to the Provisionals. The development of Provisional Sinn Fein's political strength and the election of Provisional sympathizers to local councils would not have been so successful if the H-block demonstrations had all been violent. The lengthy internal debate within the Provisional movement which preceded the August 1994 cease-fire illustrates the gulf between a strategy of violence, which some still believe might be most effective in persuading the British to 'get out', and more political and constitutional means through which Sinn Fein might be able to secure the mass electoral support which has so far eluded them. In other words, there is a tension between the Armalite *and* the ballot box, and the Armalite *versus* the ballot box.

The second main strand in the Provisionals' campaign of violence up to August 1994 consisted principally of bomb attacks on government, security and economic targets with the intention of so destabilizing the community that law and order, as enforced by the existing (British) authorities, completely broke down, the British government gave up the struggle and a demoralized loyalist community acquiesced in the establishment of a united

Ireland. These aims, together with the more immediate tactical advantages, were clearly set out by Sean MacStiofan in his memoirs, *Revolutionary in Ireland* (Saxon House, 1974), when he discussed the use of the car bomb – one of the principal weapons in the Provisionals' armoury. The car bomb, he recorded, was introduced in 1972 both for strategic and tactical reasons.

> The strategic aim was to make the government and administration of the occupied North as difficult as possible, simultaneously striking at its colonial economic structure. The British government was ultimately responsible for all compensation for bomb damage. The tactical reason was that the introduction of the car bomb tied down large numbers of British troops in the centre of Belfast and other large towns. While they were stuck there on guard duties, fewer soldiers would be available for offensive counter-insurgency operations or for harassing the people in nationalist areas under the psychological saturation policy. (p. 243)

The year 1972 was the worst year during the present troubles. There were nearly 1,400 explosions and the security forces neutralized another 500 bombs. Two attacks by the Provisionals during July demonstrated both the vulnerability of the community to car bombs and the human costs of such attacks. On 'Bloody Friday', 21 July, nineteen bombs went off in Belfast, largely without warning. Seven civilians and two soldiers were killed, while 130 people were injured. On 31 July, three car bombs exploded without warning in the village of Claudy, county Derry. Seven civilians died and twenty-nine were injured. The Provisionals have tried to explain incidents such as these by blaming British 'black' propaganda and alleged security-force delays in passing on bomb warnings, but they also admit that innocent civilians may suffer in the 'war against British imperialism'. Undoubtedly, however, attacks where there were heavy civilians casualties tended to alienate the Provisionals even from the republican community and in recent years the damage caused by car bombs – the incidence of which had in any case dropped – was mostly confined to property. Improved security procedures also reduced the impact of such attacks. Unattended parking was prohibited in most town centres and the area around public buildings was generally specially protected, although this could never be a guarantee against attack. In September 1992, for example, a 2,000 lb bomb destroyed the Northern Ireland forensic science laboratory in south Belfast and damaged 700 houses and a church.

For terrorists, the employment of car bombs reflected the weaponry available to them. Much of the explosive used in Northern Ireland was home-made, based on agricultural fertilizers, with comparatively low explosive power. Bombs were often very heavy – a 1,000-lb bomb is not uncommon – and could only be delivered to the target by vehicle. The very bulk of the explosives made it correspondingly difficult for the terrorists to store supplies. In July 1987 police discovered a ton of explosives stored in an underground steel-lined chamber on the Republic side of the border. When supplies of explosives were particularly restricted, as in 1977–8, the Provisionals might opt for fire bombs such as the blast incendiary which caused considerable damage to commercial premises in their 1977 Christmas campaign. This device consisted of a small explosive charge attached to a can of petrol which could send a ball of fire bursting into the target. In February 1978 a device such as this was detonated at the La Mon House restaurant near Comber, county Down. Twelve people were burnt to death and twenty-three seriously injured. Public reaction was so strong that the Provisionals were obliged to call off their fire-bomb campaign. Bombs, especially large ones, despite the difficulties in planting them and their frequently unpredictable results, remained an important weapon for the Provisionals since they provided the best means of scoring 'spectaculars': morale-boosting successes which attract the widest international publicity, such as the attack on Mrs Thatcher at the Grand Hotel, Brighton, in October 1984 during the Conservative Party conference.

The third strand in the Provisionals' strategy was to attack those whom they saw as the servants of British imperialism. This definition was very broadly drawn, extending as it did from full-time members of the army and police to judges and magistrates, prison officers and civilian employees of the security forces. In the mid-1980s, moreover, a particular campaign was waged against contractors working on government buildings and even shopkeepers and traders supplying goods to the army and police. Clearly attacks on senior political, diplomatic and legal figures had great attractions for the Provisionals. The Brighton bomb, the killings of the British ambassador, Christopher Ewart-Biggs, in Dublin in July 1976 and Lord Mountbatten on August Bank Holiday 1979, and that of the second most senior Northern Ireland judge, Lord Justice Gibson, in April 1987 are held by Provisionals to have been among their greatest successes as they struck at the heart of the British establishment. Bombings in England generally serve a similar purpose, although the killing of civilians, such as in the Harrods bomb in December 1983, or the Warrington bombs in March 1993 when two small boys perished, invariably provoked a hostile public reaction. The City of London bombs of 1992–3, causing damage costed at over £1000 million, marked a refinement of 'mainland' attacks, which aimed to avoid civilian casualties while hitting British economic interests especially hard.

The most regular targets for Provisional violence, however, have been members of the security forces. Over the whole period of the Troubles, up to the end of August 1994, 944 members of the security forces have died. Of these nearly half (444) were members of the regular army, while the rest came from the RUC (296) and the UDR/RIR (204). But the pattern of these casualties changed markedly over the years. In the first place the total number of security-force deaths and injuries has dropped substantially from the peak year of 1972 when 146 security personnel (and 321 civilians) died and nearly 5,000 people of all sorts were injured. Since 1982 the number of people killed has never exceeded one hundred and the *average* number of deaths (for 1983–93 inclusive) was seventy-seven. Over the same period the security-force casualties show a marked preponderance of locally-raised personnel, despite serious attacks on regular army soldiers, such as the bombing of an army bus at Ballygawley in August 1988 in which eight men died, or the bomb at Lisburn in June 1988 which killed six soldiers participating in a 'fun-run'. From 1983 to 1993 there were 75 UDR/RIR and 120 RUC deaths as opposed to 77 from the regular army. Apart from improved security procedures – the Provisionals would clearly have killed more such people if they could – this change reflected the increasing 'Ulsterization' of the security effort.

Ulsterization grew out of an official reassessment of the security effort in the mid-1970s, which mirrored a similar process within the Provisional movement. The Provisionals' strategy of the early 1970s, which aimed at a complete breakdown of government, depended on a large body of active IRA volunteers particularly in order to mobilize mass community demonstrations. This organization proved to be highly insecure and easily penetrated by the security and intelligence agencies. In 1976–7 there was a review of strategy after which the Provisionals adopted a 'long haul' approach in which a continued war of attrition against the security forces and related targets was combined with the development of an overt political organization. The IRA side of this strategy led to the adoption of a smaller and more secure cellular organization, composed of compact 'active service units'.

On the government side a working party was set up in 1976 to examine the future direction of strategy. The resulting policy contained two main strands which remained important in the following years: Ulsterization and criminalization. The abolition of internment and the 'special category status' enjoyed by para-military prisoners since mid-1972 eroded the officially-recognized distinction between 'political' and 'ordinary' crime. Nevertheless, the legal process itself effectively distinguishes between these types of crime. From 1973 terrorists (or 'scheduled') offences were dealt with in special non-jury courts. Following the imposition of direct rule in 1972, the government appointed a British judge, Lord Diplock, to head an inquiry into legal aspects of the government's response to political violence. Concerned with the intimidation of witnesses and jurors, Diplock proposed the temporary establishment of non-jury courts for the duration of the Troubles. These 'Diplock courts' still operate today. In the first instance people are tried before a judge sitting alone, while all appeals are heard before three judges. This contrasts with the situation in the Republic's non-jury courts for terrorist offences where three judges sit throughout.

The policy of Ulsterization indicated London's desire for local security forces to take on an increasing share of operations in Northern Ireland and this is reflected in the changed numerical weight of the various security forces. The number of regular army troops reached a maximum of 21,800 in July 1972. During the late 1970s there was a gradual decline and the current (mid-1995) number of soldiers stands at approximately 10,000. The size of the UDR/RIR also declined over the same period, although less dramatically. In 1972 the regiment had nearly 9,000 members. Today the locally-based element of the RIR has fewer than 6,000. But police numbers have increased, from approximately 3,000 at the beginning of the troubles to over 13,000 today. The great majority of security-force personnel are now locally raised and, indeed, live within the community itself. When off duty they represent attractive 'soft' targets for paramilitary gunmen. In the aftermath of the Anglo-Irish Agreement, too, RUC personnel living in protestant neighbourhoods (as most do) became targets of attack from loyalists bitterly opposed to the Agreement, a pattern repeated, though less intensively, in the mid-1990s, when the police enforced restrictions on some 'traditional' loyalist marches.

The denominational composition of the local security forces has had a clear impact on their effectiveness as communal peace-keepers. The UDR/RIR, which is almost entirely protestant, has frequently been characterized by nationalists as little more than a re-formed 'B' Specials, composed of ill-disciplined loyalist extremists. Certainly many former members of the Specials joined the UDR when it was first set up in 1970 and a worryingly large number of UDR personnel have been implicated in loyalist violence. Seventeen UDR men, for example, have been convicted of murder. During its life there was a very considerable turnover of personnel in the UDR with over 40,000 men and women having served in it. The army's official view is that while some unsatisfactory people have undoubtedly passed through the regiment, the current controls on recruitment and internal discipline ensure that the RIR performs its duties as impartially as possible. The RIR, in any case, is not used in all types of security duties. It is not employed for riot control and is mainly deployed in routine patrolling, manning vehicle checkpoints and guarding static installations.

Although by no means accepted as fully impartial throughout the catholic community, the RUC is regarded as a much more acceptable force than the UDR/RIR. An opinion poll taken for the *Belfast Telegraph* in early 1985 reported that 47 per cent of catholics believed that the police were performing their duties fairly. The proportion of catholics in the force has never been very high. In 1969 the number was 11 per cent. In 1993 it was revealed that just 7.7 per cent, although over 9 per cent of recruits, were catholic. The higher ranks, however, contained a rather larger proportion – over 14 per cent for chief superintendent and above. Clearly any satisfactory resolution of the security problem depends on the police being fully established as an acceptable service throughout Northern Ireland. The increasing professionalization and modernization of the force following the disasters of the late 1960s has gone a considerable way towards establishing the RUC as an impartial and widely-respected body.

With Ulsterization the chief responsibility for security has steadily been transferred to the RUC, under a policy known as 'the primacy of the police'. Since 1977 the day-to-day direction of policy has been in the hands of a security co-ordinating committee, chaired by the Chief Constable, who, in consultation with the GOC, reports to the Secretary of State. The new strategy has not been entirely trouble-free. There has been friction between army and police, and differences over the general thrust of security policy. In the summer of 1979, for example, the GOC, Sir Timothy Creasey, was arguing that 'police primacy' actually impeded an efficient security effort and that a more 'military' policy would, in the long run, prove to be more effective. The appointment of the old intelligence hand, Sir Maurice Oldfield (head of the Secret Intelligence Service, 1973–7), to be 'security co-ordinator' in October 1979 was partly in order to reduce police–army tension, but it also stemmed from the government's review of security following the assassination of Lord Mountbatten and the bomb attack at Warrenpoint which killed eighteen soldiers on 27 August 1979. Oldfield's appointment, and the arrival of new men – Sir Richard Lawson and Jack (now Sir John) Hermon – to head the army and police restored a co-operative atmosphere to the security forces. It is perhaps the case that, as an intelligence veteran, Oldfield was better qualified than a policeman or a soldier to appreciate the need for the closest possible co-ordination of the security effort. He retired in the summer of 1980 when he was succeeded by Sir Brooks Richards, who had previously been intelligence co-ordinator in the cabinet office. The post lapsed in 1981, by which time co-ordination between the different security elements had greatly improved.

With the shift in unrest away from street violence towards the more focused PIRA attacks on carefully-selected targets, the army lost most of its riot-control responsibilities and became extensively committed to covert surveillance and operational duties. The Special Air Service Regiment (SAS) has, as might be expected, provided specialist assistance in this area. Individual SAS officers helped train army-intelligence units in the early 1970s and in 1969 a squad of the regiment served in the province for a few weeks. But the regiment was not formally deployed in Northern Ireland until 1976 when, in response to an upsurge of violence in South Armagh, the prime minister, Harold Wilson, announced that SAS troops were to be employed in 'patrolling and surveillance' tasks. The SAS by their training are especially well suited for long-term covert surveillance operations, and they have served continuously in the province since 1976. It is difficult to assess the impact of these troops in Northern Ireland since information about SAS activities is mostly classified. Military opinion asserts that they have markedly assisted the security effort 'both in gathering vital information and in direct offensive operations against the IRA'. It also appears that the psychological effect of their deployment has been out of all proportion to the actual numbers of personnel involved. The popular mass media, indeed, are inclined to describe all covert army operations as 'SAS' actions, while in fact the SAS's role has largely been confined to providing training of troops from other regiments who are then deployed on what might be described as 'SAS-type' duties.

The enhanced emphasis on the covert and intelligence side of security operations has placed a particular premium on informers. In Northern Ireland in the 1980s they assumed a particular significance in the so-called 'supergrass' or converted-terrorist system. In this case the government had informers who were evidently providing a great deal of high-grade intelligence. The problem was how best this should be used. In keeping with the policy of attempting to convict as many law breakers as possible, the authorities used the information as criminal intelligence to charge and try a substantial number of suspects. Between November 1981 and November 1983 nearly 600 people were arrested on information supplied by seven loyalist and eighteen republican supergrasses. Fifteen of these informers, however, retracted their evidence and a significant number of convictions secured on uncorroborated evidence were overturned on appeal.

The overall conviction rate for the ten supergrass trials, taking appeals into account, was 44 per cent, not sufficiently high to warrant the very considerable investment of resources in the process. One informer, for example, Joseph Bennett (a former loyalist paramilitary who had been granted immunity for his own offences), was given a new name and corroborating documents by the RUC Special Branch, who also bought him a house in England and paid him a stipend. In 1986 there were reports that £30,000 had been paid to a single informer. The difficulties of using informers were embarrassingly (for the British authorities) highlighted when in January 1992 an agent, Brian Nelson, who had penetrated the loyalist UDA, was sentenced to ten years' imprisonment for offences including conspiracy to murder which he had committed while working for British military intelligence. Informers undoubtedly pose problems for the paramilitary organizations, which deal ruthlessly with suspected police agents. Apart from numerous non-fatal 'punishment shootings' (frequently in the knees), it has been calculated that the Provisionals and the INLA have 'executed' some sixty suspected informers since 1973.

In circumstances where security forces may be acquiring fairly good operational intelligence, but not of sufficient quality to use for criminal prosecutions, the authorities may be tempted to use the information either to detain suspected gunmen without trial – internment – or to inform 'special operations' against the terrorists. When internment without trial was implemented in August 1971, comparatively little was known about the recently-formed Provisionals and the information used in the initial 'sweep' was seriously out-of-date. The majority of those actually arrested (340 people) were 'old-style' republicans known for their involvement in the political side of the movement and members of the Official IRA. The Provisionals were hardly touched and the whole process was both a political and security disaster. It caused great resentment in the nationalist community and stimulated an upsurge in violence. Those actually picked up were radicalized by the experience and the internment camps themselves became 'universities of terrorism'.

From time to time allegations have been made that a 'shoot-to-kill' policy has applied in Northern Ireland. A particular illustration of this emerged through the report prepared by Mr John Stalker (Deputy Chief Constable of the Manchester Police) on the killing of six people by the security forces in November and December 1982. Five of the victims were known members of the IRA or the INLA. The sixth was an innocent 17-year-old youth, Michael Tighe. The security-force personnel responsible for the killings were attached to an RUC 'Headquarters Mobile Support Unit' (HQMSU), variously described in the press as a 'quick reaction squad', a 'SAS-trained undercover squad' and 'essentially a potential death squad'. In conjunction with a police section called 'E4A' (a covert deep surveillance unit), the HQMSUs were apparently under the general control of the Special Branch and worked closely with MI 5 and army intelligence. The Tighe killing, for example, occurred in a barn where arms were known to have been hidden and in which MI 5 technicians had planted listening devices. At the time of Tighe's death RUC and army intelligence officers were jointly monitoring these devices. The activities revealed by the Stalker inquiry demonstrate very close co-operation now between the various intelligence agencies. But they also raise questions about the command and accountability of 'special forces' which without close supervision can tend to run out of control and become a law unto themselves.

The kind of security tactics which Stalker investigated were illustrative of increasing sophistication in the security effort. It is not just the Provisionals who adopted a 'long haul' strategy. The mobilization of considerable resources – both human and technical – towards carefully gathering information about the violent challenge has become a crucial component in security policy. This side of things was undoubtedly expanded after 1992 when MI5 took on overall responsibility for heading the intelligence effort against Irish paramilitary activities in Great Britain. Long-term covert surveillance, the recruitment of informers and the systematic collation of information from a very wide range of sources can enable the security forces to strike at the Provisionals and other illegal organizations. One such notable success was achieved in May 1987 when a strong force of army and police ambushed an attack on Loughgall police station (county Armagh). Eight IRA men – the entire unit – and an innocent passing motorist were killed. These were the Provisionals' worst losses in a single incident during the troubles. The security forces – like the Provisionals for their part – could not depend on scoring many such spectacular successes. For both sides the conflict was mainly a war of attrition and no single 'military' victory brought it to a tidy finish.

The government's continued desire that terrorists may be

brought to justice through the courts indicates their appreciation of this fact. There are very considerable difficulties in marshalling enough strong evidence to secure convictions, yet in a situation where the government aims to restore the 'rule of law', there is no real alternative to working through legal channels. But the Diplock courts have come in for a very great deal of criticism from both the republican and loyalist sides, especially when the supergrass system was in operation. The issue is not so much one of the courts convicting innocent persons – there is very little evidence of this – but of the methods by which they work. It is essential, as in any free society, that justice should not only be done, but that it should be seen to be done. The streamlining of Northern Ireland's legal system to meet the difficulties presented by political violence has given rise to accusations of 'conveyor-belt justice', where the courts exist less to administer justice than to defeat terrorism. No legal system can work satisfactorily without public confidence, a point specifically recognised in the Anglo-Irish Agreement (Article 8), and the Diplock system does not command full confidence throughout the whole community.

One significant development in the 1990s was a revival of loyalist paramilitary groups who for the first time in the troubles became responsible for more killings than republicans (39 to 16 in 1992 and 48 to 36 in 1993). Although much of this activity was nakedly sectarian, the loyalists clearly felt that violence had brought the republicans political clout and might equally do so for them. Ironically, these loyalist developments owed something to security force successes. Concerns about collusion between loyalist groups and members of the security forces (especially the UDR) led to the establishment in 1989 of an enquiry under a senior British policeman, John Stevens. He found some evidence to confirm the suspicions, which led to the conviction of several UDA leaders, uncovered the informer Brian Nelson (whom we have already noted), and caused a shake-up in the loyalist organization resulting in the emergence of a new, younger, more hard-line leadership, evidently prepared to take the violent battle to the nationalist community itself.

The problem of public confidence applies with particular force to the RUC. Again this was recognized in the Anglo-Irish Agreement, which noted that 'there is a need for a programme of special measures in Northern Ireland to improve relations between the security forces and the community, with the object in particular of making the security forces more readily accepted by the nationalist community'. Following the 1994 cease-fires both the Northern Ireland Police Authority, a nominated body which had hitherto not played much of a significant role in policymaking, and Sir Hugh Annesley, Chief Constable of the RUC since 1989, launched reviews of the future role of the police. The organization, structure and even title of the police are all under consideration. Although units of the British army will for the forseeable future continue to be stationed in Northern Ireland – as was the case before 1969 – troops should only be deployed to reinforce the police in an emergency, which is the position in the rest of the United Kingdom. Northern Ireland has not quite yet returned to this desirable state of affairs, but the withdrawal of troops – including the RIR – from an active role in the province, and their replacement by ordinary police, should continue to be a government priority.

7 The International Dimension

One of the outstanding changes which has occurred with regard to Northern Ireland since 1968 is the increasing internationalization of efforts to find some way out of the conflict. The world-wide welcome for the 1985 Anglo-Irish Agreement provided manifest evidence of an international dimension to a domestic dispute in one of the world's more stable regions. It reinforced the impression created by the selling of the Agreement itself, that if there was no great enthusiasm for it in the province where the problem existed, there was no shortage of good will among well-disposed powers and even the United Nations where the then Secretary-General, Perez de Cuellar, ceremonially and simultaneously received copies from the respective British and Irish ambassadors in his headquarters within hours of the signing. On 20 December 1985 the Agreement was registered with the United Nations under Article 102 of the Charter. In the light of its dismissal by the majority of Northern Ireland's population much of this might be put down to clever public relations on the part of the various officials. Nevertheless, the presentation of the Agreement was organized by the two signatories acting in concert – an unusual enough phenomenon in the bitter and interminable saga of Anglo-Irish relations. Here, too, was proof that the Northern Ireland problem was being examined beyond 'the dreary steeples of Fermanagh and Tyrone' (to quote Winston Churchill) and with the encouragement especially of the United Kingdom. This was a remarkable advance in British attitudes since the outbreak of the Troubles. In August 1969 a joint communiqué signed by the prime ministers of the United Kingdom and of Northern Ireland affirmed that 'responsibility for affairs in Northern Ireland is entirely a matter of domestic consideration'. That was intended as a rebuff to the government of the Irish Republic which was indulging in antipartitionist rhetoric. At the United Nations, for example, the Irish foreign minister, Patrick Hillery, requested by virtue of Article 35 of the Charter 'an urgent meeting of the Security Council in connection with the situation in the *Six Counties* of Northern Ireland'. The request was rejected but the language was both emotional and deliberate: 'six counties' was meant as a diminuitive in contrast with the sovereign state of the Republic of Ireland.

If the Anglo-Irish Agreement signed at Hillsborough signalled a British concessionary mentality it must be said that the Irish Republic likewise appeared more penitent. Both the Preamble and Article 1 of the Agreement recognized the majority's right to resist Irish unity. In that respect both governments had moved a long way from the mutually hectoring and contemptuous tones of the early days of the Troubles and had adopted the 'quiet diplomacy and personal conversation' approach suggested by the then Taoiseach, Jack Lynch, when he addressed the United Nations on 22 October 1970. Arriving at that state of mind did not come easily to either side given their very long history of animosity and the vast asymmetry in relationships and political and economic development between them. But by 1980 both governments put their signatures to a communique which spoke of 'the totality of relationship within these islands'. That phrase was sufficiently vague to blur the distinction between the inter-governmental and the internal, the exogenous and endogenous.

It was also sufficiently ominous to the unionist population, and it was for that reason that Ian Paisley created his Third Force and embarked on what he called the 'Carson Trail' in self-conscious emulation of Carson's leadership in the aftermath of the Third Home Rule Bill in 1912 when the Ulster Unionists actively prepared to oppose the Westminster government with armed force. But the similarity between Paisley and Carson is only superficial. The latter had the foresight or good fortune to bring a segment of the British establishment with him; Paisley's tactics were to alienate putative support in Great Britain. Whether or not that support was forthcoming does not take away from the perennial unionist doubts about the status of the territory and regime to which they gave primary loyalty.

Following the creation of Northern Ireland in 1921 unionists engaged in enhancing their status and security. They mistrusted the original Council of Ireland suggestions (whereby the governments of Belfast and Dublin were to meet on a regular basis to deal with matters of common concern) in the Government of Ireland Act of 1920 because it held out the prospect of Irish unity. But the first prime minister, Sir James Craig (later Lord Craigavon) handled the matter with some skill when he suggested that 'in all matters under the purview of the Council' each government consult each other 'on terms of equality'. The Dublin government resisted this since it feared that it would ensure a loyalist veto, and the Council of Ireland came to naught. Instead, 'independent' Ireland refused formal recognition of the Northern entity and the new Constitution formulated by the Taoiseach, Eamon de Valera, in 1937 claimed *de jure* jurisdiction over the North. That may have been to the satisfaction of the unionist leaders because it gave them a peculiar status based on fear and grievance. In any case the unionist government had been consolidating its position within the United Kingdom. Sir James Craig had assiduously played on British disdain of all things Irish and its reluctance to get involved militarily in the Irish tangle. The result was that a relationship of mutual accommodation prevailed between the sovereign government in London and the subordinate unit in Belfast. The latter acquired a large degree of security autonomy and was more or less left to its own devices. This was to have important consequences after 1969 when the British government turned its attention to conditions in Northern

Ireland. Unionist politicians resented this interference because they misunderstood the nature of the Union. As a former prime minister, Brian Faulkner, described it, the illusions of the devolved system 'created unspoken separatist tendencies. It also meant that the crisis of 1969 hit an unprepared Westminster right between the eyes' (*Memoirs of a Statesman*, Weidenfeld and Nicolson, 1978, p. 26).

All of this has relevance to the situation which arose after 1969 and especially after 1972. One of the major opinion-formers, Enoch Powell, was convinced that every British act and attitude since 1972 – with the exception of granting Northern Ireland extra seats at Westminster in 1977 – 'has been designed to promote and facilitate the reintroduction of devolution in a form which could be moved or pressured into a direct relationship with the Republic . . . sweetened by a British Isles totality or a Commonwealth or an EEC or a NATO dimension' because Britain is convinced that 'the island of Ireland is vital to the "defence of the West" '. Powell unveiled this plot in the *Spectator* (8 January 1983) where he delineated the principles that guide Britain, Ireland and the USA to tease out a solution based on Irish unity. He asserts that the strategy is based on four principles: (i) the Republic cannot take Northern Ireland by force; (ii) to end partition there needs to be an autonomous Ulster with 'guarantees' in a federal Ireland, possibly in some loose relationship with Britain; (iii) United Kingdom pressure is necessary to accomplish this; but (iv) that will be exerted only when Irish unity is 'strategically necessary to Britain. The key lies in the 'defence of the West'. In numerous speeches he strove to reveal the United States' unwelcome interference in Northern Ireland's affairs. It is not our purpose to judge the validity of these claims, and in any case conspiracy theories are not easy to prove. But there can be little doubt that the international plane has taken on an added dimension as the Troubles have proceeded.

A favourite ploy of Irish diplomats in the earlier years of partition was 'to raise the sore thumb' – that is, to complain about the malign effects of partition on Ireland's development at every opportune moment during international gatherings. This procedure was based on the false premise that if Irish statesmen publicised the wrongs their country had suffered, the world would come to their assistance. That strain in Irish foreign policy has a reasonable lineage stretching back to an American tour by Eamon de Valera in 1919. Surprisingly, when the Troubles did break out the Irish used the ploy less than some might have anticipated. With the exception of the famous piece of shadow boxing between the foreign affairs minister, Patrick Hillery, and the British ambassador to the United Nations, Lord Caradon, at the UN in August 1969, and the hiring of an international public relations firm for a short period, Ireland did not indulge in this tactic. It preferred to deal directly with the British government.

One possible reason was that it was embarrassed by its own unpreparedness for the North's political violence. This was at least something it shared with London. Its level of knowledge and expertise concerning the North was abysmal – a factor which might be explained by the anomalous relationship which existed between Dublin and London for many years. Although Ireland had left the Commonwealth in 1949, as late as 1968 it was located in the British *Diplomatic Service List* under 'List of British Representatives in the Commonwealth, and the Republic of Ireland'. It seemed to enjoy a unique status, neither part of the British Commonwealth of Nations nor wholly 'foreign'. Had it been the latter then the Foreign Office would have been expected to have provided the 'amassed and living knowledge of overseas countries' which is its special contribution to the national effort. There simply was no amassed and living knowledge regarding Ireland. Until 1965, when the Foreign and Commonwealth Services were amalgamated, the British Embassy in Dublin was staffed by the Commonwealth Service and reported (until October 1968) to the Commonwealth Office. According to Sir John Peck, who was appointed ambassador in April 1970, this had a disastrous effect since during

the first fifteen months of responsibility for relations with the
Republic of Ireland, the staff of the Foreign Office had discovered
that they knew very little about it. The reason was that the
traditions and requirements of the Foreign Office and the
Commonwealth Office had been different. The Foreign Office
dealt with a world that is truly foreign – independent nations
which might be stronger or weaker than Britain, friendly or hostile,
but which were in any case wholly detached. The Commonwealth
Office dealt with former British colonies . . . where, as befits a
member of the family, a good deal could be taken for granted.
(*Dublin from Downing Street*, Gill and Macmillan, 1978, p. 17)

But nothing could be taken for granted in Anglo-Irish relations.

The anomaly had arisen with Eire's decision to leave the
Commonwealth. Cabinet papers for 1948 reveal the British
government's uncertainty as to how to handle the position.
Initially it was decided that the Republic of Ireland (as it
became known) would be treated like any other foreign state.
But, after conferring with some of the Commonwealth leaders,
the decision was reversed. Apart from anything else, there were
practical difficulties for the Home Office which would have faced
formidable administrative problems if all Irish citizens had to be
treated as aliens. There were also fears that the Republic would
be in a strong position to put pressure on the UK at the United
Nations if it raised the question of partition at the General
Assembly, where it would be assured of considerable support.
Britain, too, would be embarrassed if it had to give positive
support to the continuance of partition. So, for practical, strategic
and expedient reasons it would be better if it were assumed that
Ireland were still 'family'. Ireland appeared to go along with this
diplomatic fiction which was mutually advantageous as long as
the North did not explode. Once it did all bets were off.

This explains that lack of preparedness, a problem which
was compounded as the volume of work on Ireland increased
substantially. An administrative decision that a newly created
Republic of Ireland department within the Foreign Office should
report to an under-secretary whose principal concern was Defence

and Foreign Office liaison with the Service departments had inevitable consequences because, to quote Peck, it 'introduced the danger that departmental advice reaching the Foreign Secretary about policy towards the Republic would be related primarily to our military policy and interests in the domestic law and order situation in the North' (*Dublin from Downing Street*, p. 116). Here we have the full complexity of the Northern Ireland problem unfolding. For unionists it was entirely an internal affair to be sorted out by a strict security policy or perhaps by tinkering with reforms. But the Foreign Office was becoming conscious of its external dimension and of its potential for embarrassment abroad.

None of this was of any great moment in 1969, and indeed it might be argued that not until 1976 or 1977 that playing the American card became significant. The reason, paradoxically, concerned the failure of political movement in Northern Ireland itself. The events by which the powersharing government was brought down and the lack of generosity in the convention report convinced the SDLP that it would have to seek its salvation elsewhere. At its annual conference in 1977 the party adopted a more green policy when it emphasized the Irish dimension and called on the British government to spell out its long-term intentions for Northern Ireland. John Hume, then deputy leader, shifted strategy on to the international plane in an attempt to concentrate the official mind. His party adopted a threefold strategy: (i) to discourage Irish-Americans from contributing to Provisional IRA funds, (ii) to link substantial US aid to economic development in Northern Ireland if an acceptable political solution could be found and (iii) to involve the presidency in seeking out an Irish policy.

All of this seemed to come into play on 30 August 1977 when US president Jimmy Carter made a seven-paragraph statement which condemned violence and made a promise of economic aid in the event of a political solution being found. While the statement did say that there 'are no solutions that outsiders can impose' it has been recognized as going beyond America's benign neutrality in this matter and it displays an element of impatience with the lack of political movement in the province. Its publication denoted both that the Irish lobby in Washington was becoming influential and also that British interests in the United States conceded as much.

One of the features of Irish America has been its disintegrative tendency. Unlike other ethnic lobbies there has been no co-ordinated effort from the Irish simply because there is the same fundamental split as at home between constitutional and physical-force nationalists. The Irish Northern Aid Committee, more popularly known as Noraid, has been in existence since April 1970 as a fundraiser and money supplier to the IRA, although it has claimed that its resources only go to the families of imprisoned IRA personnel. One knowledgeable commentator, Jack Holland (author of *The American Connection: United States Guns, Money and Influence in Northern Ireland* (Viking Penguin, 1987)), has estimated that at one time it had seventy units throughout the United States and 2,000 members in New York alone. It may have raised as much as $10 million since 1971 for the cause, so there can be little doubt that it has been of considerable benefit to the Provisional effort. Since the ceasefire, however, Noraid support has been considerably reduced. The organization shares the militant platform with a number of other groups some of which may not condone IRA violence but all of which believe that the answer to the problem of Northern Ireland is British withdrawal. These included the Ad Hoc Committee on Irish Affairs set up by Congressman Mario Biaggi in September 1977 to press for congressional hearings on the problem. Until 1988 when he was jailed for corruption offences (unconnected with Ireland) Biaggi could muster as many as 120 congressional signatures on motions critical of British government policy although the number of active members of his Ad Hoc group was never more than about ten. At the very least he could act as an extreme irritant and he was suspected by the Irish government of being a closet supporter of violence. A third group worthy of mention is the Irish National Caucus led by Father Sean McManus. It is a professional lobbying organization with offices on Capitol Hill in Washington and an impressive self-publicist in its director. Father McManus has stressed that the Northern Ireland problem is an American issue and in that respect no Irish government nor Irish politician can dictate to Irish-Americans how they should conduct their campaign. It follows that there is not much love lost between the Caucus and successive Irish governments. Indeed, even across the militant platform there are differences of personality and of strategy so that in combination they are not as powerful as their potential would suggest.

That may be one reason why the constitutionalists gathered together in the Friends of Ireland group. It is much smaller than the Ad Hoc committee but much more influential. The Friends evolved out of what was known as the 'Four Horsemen' who were Senators Ted Kennedy and Patrick Moynihan, the late House Speaker 'Tip' O'Neill and former governor of New York Hugh Carey. These four wielded huge influence in their own right so that any joint statement from them had to be taken with the utmost seriousness. At the start of the Troubles some of their remarks were highly emotional and based on lack of information. But with the support of the Irish Embassy in Washington and certain politicians, notably John Hume, they began to move beyond the simple 'Brits Out' kneejerk reaction to something more considered and constructive. Their annual St Patrick's Day statement became something of a ritual and a barometer of Irish constitutionalism's standing in America. Significantly, they devoted considerable effort in unambivalent condemnation of IRA and other violence so that the attitude of the British Embassy and governments became much more positive towards them. In that respect the British looked forward to these statements as one possible means to diminish republican support in Ireland. Unobtrusively, therefore, that which had been purely a matter of domestic consideration was now being seen as one in which Irish America had a role to play. But there was also an *American* domestic dimension to the situation. Well-organized Irish-American pressure groups have intermittently suceeded in placing the question of Northern Ireland on the United States political agenda. Bill Clinton deliberately courted Irish-American opinion during his 1992 presidential election campaign, and he has been actively interventionist with regard to Ireland party because it is a foreign policy issue where success might bring domestic political gains for him.

One problem which the constitutional nationalists had to face was that their support came solely from the Democrats. The day might arise when the Republican Party controlled Congress and the Presidency and Kennedy and company would have a much diminished role. Hence the move to establish the Friends with much more widespread support. It was formally launched in 1981 when a Republican, Ronald Reagan, was in the White House. But the President had to work closely with the House Speaker, Tip O'Neill. Their coincidence of Irish background enabled them to work in some harmony on this particular issue. In the meantime the Friends had recruited twenty members from the Senate and twenty-one from the House of Representatives.

If President Carter's August 1977 statement can be seen as establishing that the problem of Northern Ireland was a legitimate subject for concern in American foreign policy the implications did not manifest themselves for a few years. In April 1979 in the run-up to the British general election Tip O'Neill on a visit to Ireland made some very pointed remarks about the lack of political movement in Northern Ireland and the propensity of Westminster politicians to treat it like a political football. These remarks were considered to be gross interference in the British jurisdiction and the Speaker had to endure the wrath of Fleet Street tabloid leader writers. Nevertheless his remarks were taken seriously by the incoming prime minister, Margaret Thatcher. In her first major interview for a foreign newspaper (*New York Times*, 12 November 1979) the prime minister made no secret of her impatience: 'We will listen for a while. We hope we will get agreement. But then the Government will have to make some decisions and say "having listened to everyone, we are going ahead to try this or that" whichever we get most support for'. They went ahead with what became known as the Atkins initiative, an effort by the new secretary of state to devise another devolved Assembly with the assistance of the indigenous politicians. This sounded suspiciously like what Speaker O'Neill had demanded in April 1979 – 'an early, realistic and major initiative on the part of the incoming British government so as to get negotiations moving quickly'. That Atkins did not succeed was not altogether surprising and lack of success may even have given a stimulus to the Anglo-Irish process which got under way with two summits, May and December, in 1980.

It is the strongly held belief of some unionists that this process is part of a wider strategy. Enoch Powell, for example, has described the Foreign Office as 'the inveterate enemy of the Union' and the summit talks as part of a plan to abolish Northern Ireland and incorporate the unified country inside NATO. The beneficiary would be the United States since it would block 'the gravest of all the gaps in the American strategy for Europe'. This conspiracy theory was put at greater length by the Ulster Unionist leader, Jim Molyneaux, in a Northern Ireland Assembly debate on 22 March 1983 when he revealed that a 'high powered conference took place in London between the British and American Governments' some weeks after the Conservatives came back into power in 1979 in which Northern Ireland affairs were discussed between Lord Carrington and secretary of state, Cyrus Vance (contrary to the declarations of successive British governments) to the effect that the internal affairs of the United Kingdom were a matter for the UK government and Parliament. Mr Molyneaux's suspicions may well have been fuelled by the rapidity with which British policy had changed. As late as 5 May 1978 the British and Irish governments issued a joint statement in Dublin which said *inter alia*: 'The British and Irish Governments have a different approach in the search for a long-term solution for peace and stability in Northern Ireland'. Yet two years later they embarked on a process which was to culminate in the Anglo-Irish Agreement and which was to be endorsed happily by the American administration.

There may, however, be simpler explanations. There can be little doubt that the Reagan administration invested much time and money in countering the network of international terrorism. One of his most ardent supporters in that and other policies has been Mrs Thatcher. It may be asserted that Irish terrorist organizations do not play a notable role on the international scene but, given that it is acknowledged that IRA funding comes from the United States, it would be surprising if the two leaders did not co-operate in this sphere. And if the job is to be done thoroughly then the assistance of the Irish authorities is called for, something which is recognized in the Anglo-Irish Agreement.

A second explanation predates President Reagan. It is the concern for human rights issues enunciated by President Carter, an issue taken more seriously by Democrat than Republican presidents, hence the renewed interest shown by the Clinton administration. Irish Americans were not slow in drawing attention to what they perceived as the lack of certain rights in Northern Ireland. These included the most fundamental such as the Provisional claim to the right to self-determination whereby the people of the island of Ireland should settle its constitutional destiny. At a more mundane but very emotive level they included charges of judicial prejudice and job discrimination against the catholic minority. Thus there was the sustained campaign against an extradition bill involving the UK and USA which would have enabled the American authorities to return suspected IRA terrorists to the British jurisdiction for trial. The campaign to block the bill received widespread publicity because it was being fought out at the Senate Foreign Relations Committee level. Although this campaign was ultimately unsuccessful, with the 1986 UK–USA Extradition Treaty allowing the arrest and return of IRA suspects, at the level of state legislatures the battle continued over the MacBride principles. All of this gives publicity to the Irish cause and has managed to embarrass both the British and American authorities from time to time. It is inevitable that in a society as highly tuned to the professional lobbyist as the United States these issues play a more dominant part than they would in Britain.

In these circumstances there need not be any sinister motives for the relatively keen interest taken by the most powerful state in the world. The kinship network on both sides of the divide and the willingness of both Britain and Ireland to work in harmony produce conditions which permit the US to get involved. One way in which this has been demonstrated is in US government funding to assist economic development and thus improve social conditions in Northern Ireland. Between 1985 and 1993 some $120 million of American aid was granted for distribution through the International Fund for Ireland.

Human rights have also played a part in provoking greater European involvement. On 16 December 1971 the Irish government filed with the European Commission on Human Rights an interstate application in accordance with Article 24 of the European Convention for the Protection of Human Rights and Fundamental Freedoms concerned with the treatment of a number of internees. It was not adopted until 25 January 1976. The Irish were able to claim a victory of sorts but there was little doubt that the matter had created animosity between the two states. In general Ireland used 'Europe' in a less controversial manner although that was not the way it was viewed by loyalists. Document 3696, for example, which was debated before the Council of Europe on 29 January 1976 affirmed that

> just as there is an Irish dimension . . . there is a European dimension which can be seen at three different levels (a) British and Irish membership of the Council . . . established, inter alia, to guarantee the principle of democracy and human rights . . . thus [it would be] inconsistent if that organisation did not consider the problem of Northern Ireland as a common European experience (b) the Council of Europe has an interest in matters concerning legislation, and the administration and judicial practices obtaining in Northern Ireland (c) common membership of the EEC which imposed upon them an even higher degree of obligation to cooperate than is the case between sovereign states in general.

The document came down unequivocally in favour of 'strong coalition government' which should develop 'technical, social and economic' co-operation between North and South. It was unanimously approved by the Political Affairs Committee.

The Council of Europe did not carry too much weight and it is doubtful if the document made any significant impact. The same could not be said, however, for the Haagerup Report, drawn up for the European Parliament by a Danish MEP, Neils Haagerup. Initially his appointment was opposed in Britain on the grounds that any investigation would be an unwarranted interference in the internal affairs of the United Kingdom, but when the report was published British Conservatives abstained in the European Parliament rather than vote against it as many of them had been urged. This might suggest a more enlightened and broad attitude than hitherto, because while the preamble to the report accepted that 'the European Community has no competence to make proposals for changes in the Constitution of Northern Ireland', none the less it did make several interesting suggestions. It called, for example, for the Community to assume greater responsibility for the economic and social development of the province; it encouraged closer Anglo-Irish co-operation and a powersharing form of government in Northern Ireland. The muted British response was surprising and it may be interpreted as an acceptance that solutions to the problem were to be found in a broader context than merely within the province. After all, Haagerup was published in 1984, prior to the New Ireland Forum Report and as the Anglo-Irish process was gathering momentum.

It was possible, however, to construe the Haagerup Report as part of a carefully devised pattern. The tenor of his remarks added fuel to the conspiracy theories. It was noticeable that the most articulate unionist spokesman, Enoch Powell, was also vehemently against the UK joining the European Community (now the European Union). One of the reasons, moreover, why the Republic sought membership was the belief that accession could create a more positive Anglo-Irish outlook through the theme of functional co-operation. The psychological impact on the Republic may have been such that it began to see itself as a

co-ordinate and not subordinate unit in the islands. It meant that
Anglo-Irish relations were not quite so obsessional a part of Irish
foreign policy as they had been at the start of the 1970s. And if
one looks at Irish trading figures since entry there has been a
significant shift away from the almost total dependence on the
British market.

But there were political overtones. The European Commission's
decision to designate the entire island of Ireland as a single region
in the planning of regional policy produced the following reaction
from Mr Powell. Speaking in December 1976 he declared that
those who supposed that on the continent of Europe there would
be either sympathy of understanding or patience for the million
British subjects in Ulster who obstinately affirm they are part of
the United Kingdom know nothing about Europe and Europeans.
'As the member states are absorbed into the new European State as
provinces' he predicted, 'I will tell you what one of those provinces
will be. It will be the Province of Ireland, already the official name
for the Irish Republic in the documents and language of the
EEC.' That was speculation. The reality has been that European
integration has been much slower than its architects intended, and
only the most starry-eyed optimists now look forward to proper
political integration. Indeed, one of the stumbling blocks has been
the Republic's insistence that it is a neutral country. This is not
the place to examine the validity of that claim, simply to report
its capability to impede political integration. Similarly, Ireland's
decision to enter the European Monetary System (EMS) in 1979
and Britain's decision to remain outside has had the inevitable
consequence of widening the division between North and South.
Before EMS entry both parts of Ireland enjoyed the same currency
arrangements, but now that the Irish 'punt' has become part of
the European basket its rate of exchange fluctuates with that of
sterling, thereby strengthening the symbolism of the border.

Europe, nevertheless, remains an important component, at times
drawing the conflicting parties in Northern Ireland together.
As part of an economically disadvantaged peripheral region,
Ireland, North and South, has attracted substantial amounts of

European Union (EU) development funds. Cross-border schemes are particularly encouraged and politicians representing both nationalists and unionists frequently co-operate in the quest for such funding. In mid-1995 the EU promised a £240 'peace aid package' to be disbursed in Northern Ireland and border counties of the Republic. Europe has unquestionably become part of the political context of the 'Northern Ireland problem'. The Downing Street Declaration of December 1993 emphasized that 'the development of Europe' would require 'new approaches' to serve common interests within the island of Ireland and between Ireland and the United Kingdom 'as partners in the European Union'.

Another factor, at least in the early days of the Troubles, was the deployment of large numbers of the British army in close proximity to a land border which stretches for over 300 miles. Their presence created tensions which might have provoked an international incident. The Irish complained, for example, of forty-seven border incursions and twenty-seven overflights by the British between August 1969 and early 1972. In a special Dail debate in October 1971 the Taoiseach, Mr Lynch, warned that 'if there are repeated and more serious incursions by the British army across the border it may be necessary to seize the U.N. of this issue as a threat to international peace'.

The international dimension, therefore, could be either benign or malign but probably not neutral. Certainly from early on the Irish recognized, sometimes naïvely, its positive features. Even before European accession the Taoiseach was offering the unionist prime minister Brian Faulkner the availability of Ireland's collective experience and knowledge of European affairs. The offer was accepted in principle and talks at senior-official level were initiated. Garret FitzGerald, as Minister for Foreign Affairs after March 1973, went so far as to promote the regional fund interest of both North and South at a council of ministers meeting in November 1974. He was to be rebutted by both the British government and by unionist politicians. Fianna Fail ministers played the same card when they came back into office after

1977. Michael O'Kennedy went on the offensive in 1979 when he described Northern Ireland as 'the last remaining problem in the Community for peace, it is an exception to the pattern in the rest of the EEC. *The goodwill in Europe and the United States is there to be tapped to support a return to normal politics in the North*'.

Beyond the European and American dimensions the picture has been patchy. Only two international statesmen, both of whom fused temporal positions with spiritual leadership, Pope Paul VI and Archbishop Makarios, dared to speak of Irish unity. Others were more controversial: the Chilean dictator, President Pinochet, expressed concern at the existence of concentration camps in Ulster, and the Ugandan leader, Idi Amin, once demanded a briefing in Northern Ireland from the British High Commissioner in Kampala.

All of this is simply to say that there was and is an international dimension, but that its positive qualities were largely ignored until the signing of the Anglo-Irish Agreement. It is not too difficult to see why it had not come into play much earlier. From a British perspective, to acknowledge the dimension was to accept that Northern Ireland was not a purely internal affair. Unionists were inclined to see it as gross interference and even as a Popish plot and in any case not to the advantage of the loyalist population. The international community, singly or collectively, was reluctant to intervene in a dispute between two friendly powers, other than to offer whatever humanitarian assistance it could muster. There was, too, the well-recognized principle of sovereignty whereby one did not intervene in another's grief. Besides no state was without its blemishes and would not want these held up before the international community. Ireland was learning to come to terms with the nature of the problem for many years before it could even contemplate organizing others in a systematic manner on its behalf.

Much of that is past history. The position remains that any support for reconciliation from outside the archipelago has to be construed as constructive and not interference. The potential for such constructive co-operation should not be underestimated.

8 Politics as Process

In the summer of 1994 a well-crafted mural appeared in the Bogside district of Derry. It depicted a British army squaddie holding aloft a Union Jack marching down the road signposted 'London'. The caption read 'Slan Abhaile' – roughly translated as 'Safe Home'. The message was seductively simple. The 'war' was over and the implication was that 'victory' had been secured against the British. The use of the Irish language reinforced the sense of communal solidarity against alien forces. The timing was appropriate, too, because the troops had arrived on the streets of Derry exactly twenty-five years earlier in a bid to hold the peace. In the interim there had been approximately 3,400 conflict-related deaths; and the financial subvention from the United Kingdom Treasury had risen from £73 million in 1969–70 to £3 billion by 1994. The price of keeping the peace was not inconsiderable.

When the Army arrived in large numbers in 1969 commentators speculated that it would take between three to six months to clear up what cabinet minister Richard Crossman called 'the most messy kind of civil war one has ever seen'. Soon it became evident that the problem did not fit into the usual parameters of British political practice because 'in Ulster, the great permanent questions of political philosophy – the moral basis of authority, and of the right to resist authority, the relationship between law and force and that between nationality and political allegiance – were being debated' (T. E. Utley, *Lessons of Ulster*, Dent 1975, p. 7). That debate has gone on ever since. Some believe that it is reaching a satisfactory conclusion, and place their optimism in the peace process. This chapter will outline the nature of that process by placing it in the context of the relationship between politics and violence.

One of the intended side-effects of the Anglo-Irish Agreement was to produce fluidity and flexibility within and between the province's political parties. That was slow in coming. The unionist slogan 'Ulster Says No' encapsulates stagnation on the political landscape. Unionists were not prepared to work the levers of power – save using local councils and Westminster as sniping positions – until the Agreement was brought to the point of ignominious collapse. Extra-parliamentary protest became the argot of political discourse. Large-scale demonstrations were the means implemented to convey loyalist anger. On the wilder shores new groups (such as Ulster Resistance) emerged and the level of loyalist paramilitary killing increased incrementally. In 1984 fewer than ten deaths were ascribed to loyalist groups. In the period 1988–90 they claimed an annual average of twenty victims and in both 1991 and 1992 double that number died.

Yet there were some stirrings in the political undergrowth. The Ulster Political Research Group's pamphlet *Common Sense* in January 1987 has already been noted. Its impact was such that it goaded the mainstream unionist parties into seeking positive alternatives to the Anglo-Irish Agreement. The first fruits of this process was the publication in July 1987 of a 'Task Force Report', *An End To Drift*, produced by three senior members of the DUP and UUP on the state of unionist opinion. The report recognized the 'inadequacies of the existing campaign (against the Agreement); the 'limits of Unionism's negotiating strength'; and that 'membership of the United Kingdom or membership of an Irish Republic are *not* the only options available to the people of Northern Ireland'. In the meantime the secretary of state, Tom King, had initiated a series of 'talks about talks' among the parties. All of that may have induced a *little* realism because the Unionist joint manifesto for the June 1987 general election sought to 'ascertain whether the new government is prepared to create the circumstances and conditions necessary to encourage successful negotiation including the suspension of the workings of the Agreement and of the Maryfield Secretariat'.

The government were not prepared to go that far and did not reveal their hand fully until their May 1989 review of the Agreement. It stated (in the penultimate paragraph) that both governments were prepared to contemplate 'changes in the scope and nature of the [Anglo-Irish] Conference' provided that these were 'consistent with the basic provisions and spirit of the Agreement'. In any case other pressures were coming to bear on unionism's negotiating manoeuvres, one a negative and one a positive. The negative concerned Fianna Fail's stance. It had been extremely hostile to the Agreement in opposition and there was an assumption that it would undermine it if it got into office. But pragmatism triumphed when it returned to power in 1987 with the result that unionism and republicanism were isolated in their opposition to the Agreement. The positive was the attitude of SDLP leader John Hume. He started to convey the message that the Agreement was not written on tablets of stone and that it could be replaced by another Agreement which transcended it in importance. All of these factors encouraged exploration on the scope and nature of political change.

The unlikely emissary of change was Peter Brooke, appointed secretary of state in July 1989. He appeared somewhat Bertie Woosterish and not the man for the mean streets of Belfast and Derry. Little political movement was expected. The 'Review of the Working of the Conference' suggested that both governments were comfortable with the status-quo and that they would raise the levels of functional co-operation. Sinn Fein's electoral drive had been contained in the years following the Agreement and the SDLP appeared at ease with itself. Unionism remained in a state of paralysis. Yet by the time Mr Brooke left Northern Ireland in April 1992 he had moved matters on considerably. An early indication of his political intent surfaced after 100 days in office when he stated that an abandonment of IRA violence could lead to 'imaginative steps' by the government.

In another speech made on 9 November 1989 he claimed that the British had no economic or strategic interest in the union; that it would accept unification by consent; and that there would be a place for non-violent republicanism. Neither of these speeches made any great impact at the time – although Sinn Fein's Martin McGuinness had described him as the first secretary of state 'with some understanding of Irish history' – but, with hindsight, they may amount to one of the defining moments in contemporary Anglo-Irish relations. Commentators concentrated on style rather than substance. They underestimated a carefully cultivated sense of bewilderment and a delivery based on understatement.

Both of these were in evidence in two speeches addressed at unionism. On 6 December he declared that he had 'no secret plan, no hidden agenda'; and he advised Bangor Chamber of Commerce on 9 January 1990: 'I would not wish to raise hopes unduly'. While neither amounted to a modern version of the Gettysburg Address, the Bangor speech can be seen as the beginning of what is called the Brooke initiative. It was posited on finding something positive to say about the major political parties and on rescuing unionism from its 'internal exile'. The initiative was to be about creating conditions which would enable the Agreement to be replaced by something which would embrace *all* the parties to the problem.

As we have seen he was not entirely alone when he set out on his journey in January 1990. Three concessions – made with the acquiescence of the SDLP and the Irish government – were enough to bring the UUP and DUP into the process. He allowed that he was prepared to consider an alternative to the Agreement. He had agreed to a predetermined gap between meetings of the intergovernmental conference to allow talks to get under way. And he suggested that during these talks officials in the Anglo-Irish Secretariat could be gainfully employed elsewhere. All of this was contributing to a subtle shift in the political vocabulary back towards the 'totality of relationships', a phrase which first was used in an Anglo-Irish summit way back in 1980. In his Bangor speech he had referred to the three relationships – the intercommunity and British / Irish dimensions as well as north / south relations. Now he needed to put some flesh on the concept.

Over the next six months he believed that he had reached an understanding with the constitutional parties and hoped to make a Commons statement before the summer recess. But he was blocked by the SDLP/Dublin axis unhappy with two substantive points. They wanted to know when the talks would move from Strand 1 (talks within Northern Ireland) to Strand 2 (north/south talks). They suspected that unionist insistence on 'substantial progress' on the talks internal to Northern Ireland would allow for procrastination and would assist them in avoiding direct talks with Dublin. In addition they were unhappy with unionists attending Strand 2 as part of a UK delegation since they believed that unionism's relations with the rest of the island went to the heart of the conflict.

Secondly Dublin alleged that Mr Brooke had gone back on an agreement made on 19 April when it was claimed, agreement had been reached that the talks would proceed 'in unison'. This type of hiccup was typical of the procedural debate. It was not entirely unexpected since the parties were dealing with a very complex problem and all were carrying the burden of history with them. Talks recommenced in the autumn but it was not until 26 March 1991 that Mr Brooke announced that the intergovernmental meetings would be suspended for a period of about ten weeks from mid-April for bilateral talks to set an agenda. This would be followed by Strand 1 involving the UUP, DUP, Alliance Party and SDLP; Strand 2 talks between the Northern Ireland parties and the Irish government; and Strand 3 dealing with east/west or London/Dublin relations. Everyone recognized the historic import of these talks and the proactive role played by Mr Brooke in getting them to that point – DUP leader, Ian Paisley, praised him for conducting his dealings 'in honesty, uprightness and with great openness'. But that was to be the end of the courtship because the talks ran into a whole series of problems not all of which will be rehearsed here. Instead we will examine the major themes and difficulties which occurred in the Brooke and (following the April 1992 general election) Mayhew talks. They can be categorized loosely around questions of procedure and of symbolism.

The Dublin input was the major problem for unionists: when would it become part of the proceedings? Where were meetings to be held? Who was to chair them? An early decision was taken that Mr Brooke would decide when the Irish government joined the process. In the meantime talks were to begin on 30 April with a series of bilateral meetings between the NIO and party leaders to finalise house keeping arrangements such as location and the length and frequency of interparty talks. These bilaterals were to be 'fairly brisk' so that such issues could be dealt with in the margins. But location proved to be such a stumbling block that the first plenary session did not take place until 17 June; and the whole process had collapsed by 2 July when Mr Brooke decided to bring them to a close to avoid any further recrimination.

Essentially the talks did not move to the substantive (beyond well-rehearsed party positions). The question of location concerned Strand 2. The SDLP wanted it on Irish soil whereas unionists refused to sit down with an Irish government *in Ireland* unless Articles 2 and 3 of the Irish Constitution were rescinded or amended. (Gerry Adams offered a novel venue – SF headquarters in Belfast was available!) Dublin had assumed that Irish Foreign Minister, Gerry Collins, would chair the second strand and was prepared to rotate it between him and Mr Brooke. Unionists wanted only the latter but were prepared eventually to accept an independent chairman. They were scandalized by the first choice of Lord Carrington: 'his record on Northern Ireland is deplorable . . . His remarks about unionists have been disparaging and offensive', according to a statement from the two unionist leaders on 29 May. Eventually, after scouring the world and considering about thirty names, the government settled on a former Governor-General of

Australia, Sir Ninian Stephen. In the event he neither visited Northern Ireland nor chaired a session during the Brooke talks. When the secretary of state told Parliament on 20 June that the intergovernmental Conference would be held on schedule on 16 July the talks were effectively at an end. It was clear that they could not cover all three strands in the limited time available. The SDLP had not placed their specific proposals on the future governance of Northern Ireland on the table because they feared they would be leaked during the highly emotive marching season. The unionist parties would not contemplate another gap between Conferences after 16 July. Even in these circumstances Mr Brooke refused to be downhearted. On 3 July he told the Commons that 'foundations had been laid for progress in the future which neither cynics nor men of violence will be able to undermine'. He hoped to pick up the process in the autumn. In fact serious talks did not recommence until the following spring under a new secretary of state, Sir Patrick Mayhew.

Nonetheless the Brooke initiative had been important for several reasons. In the first place it established that the problem could be settled only in terms of the three strands; and as a significant addendum Peter Brooke had introduced a safety net in a parliamentary statement on 14 May 1991 that 'nothing will be finally agreed in any strand until everything is agreed on the talks as a whole'. Secondly it was an educational experience for all concerned. The NIO came face to face with the role of symbolism in Irish politics. The local parties were being tutored in the art of political negotiation; some trust had been created. There were those, however, who insisted on feeding on paranoia – the unionist daily, the *Newsletter* (31 May 1991) cautioned that the NIO had manipulated sections of the media by selling 'the talks as being synonymous with peace. It may be nearer the mark to say that they are synonymous with movement towards a united Ireland.'

The Mayhew Talks

Sir Patrick Mayhew enjoyed several advantages unavailable to his predecessor. The Brooke initiative had established a momentum of its own, one which was shared by the general public. An opinion poll commissioned by the Rowntree Reform Trust in Britain, Ireland and Northern Ireland and published on 12 July 1991 found that 80 per cent of the electorate wanted the talks to continue 'as soon as possible' because they 'were potentially vital to the future of Northern Ireland'. Brooke, too, had provided a kind of catharsis involving retreat from previously stated positions to less 'extreme' positions as perceived by the adversaries; and the debilitating procedural discussions were now behind all the parties.

Following a meeting of the Anglo-Irish Conference on 27 April the governments had agreed to a three-month suspension to allow the talks to proceed. This was a longer period than the corresponding break a year earlier – but then Ian Paisley had complained that 'injury time' should have been built into the Brooke talks. Sir Patrick was adamant that 'three months means what it says. This is not a case of "oh, we will come back for more later".' In fact, with the exception of a short summer break, the talks ran on until 10 November. Although the secretary of state said that he approached the talks with 'no blueprint' he had intimated that he would leave the talks with Northern Ireland still an integral part of the UK. In turn even before the process got under way the Irish Foreign Minister, David Andrews, announced, 'If Articles 2 and 3 or our constitution are up for discussion, is there any reason other constitutional positions are not up for discussion?' And so it proved to be. Mayhew got bogged down on final status issues – such as sovereignty and territoriality – rather than transitional questions which would have allowed for a more modest approach.

The talks began formally on 29 April 1992 (coincidentally the date for the opening of the Brooke talks the previous year) and initially moved at a brisk pace. Strand 1 got under way on 9 May, Strand 2 on 6 July, and Strand 3 on 28 July. Another feature was the displacement of symbolic hurdles. For example, when the parties met together at Lancaster House in London for the beginning of Strand 2 it was the first time in 70 years that all of them had sat down together (and in a building where the Rhodesia/Zimbabwe negotiations had taken place); when four Irish ministers travelled to Belfast for a further meeting on 15 July they were doing so at the height of the Orange marching season; and when Jim Molyneaux led his UUP team to the talks in Dublin in September he displayed political courage and, it should be said, astuteness – in that he read the mind of the unionist community more sensitively than his DUP rival, Ian Paisley.

If any one issue illustrated the fundamental distance between the Northern Ireland parties it was the leaking of a radical document from the SDLP on 11 May. The SDLP suggested that the province be governed by a Northern Ireland Executive Commission of six members, three of whom would be elected within Northern Ireland with the remainder appointed by Dublin, London and the EC to encompass 'the totality of relationships within these islands': 'the Commission would reflect both the democratic preferences of the electorate in Northern Ireland and the key external relationships which it is necessary to cater for, since they are no less fundamental to agreeing internal relationships in Northern Ireland than they are to external aspects'. Little reference was made to the relations between the Commission and a proposed Northern Ireland Assembly or Westminster; much of the detail would have to await the other two strands 'because of their implication for the wider relationship'.

The SDLP document is interesting because, while it was tabled in Strand 1, it transcended all three strands. Secondly, it ensured that the wider dimension was now part of the political discourse – despite the annoyance of the unionist parties. Thirdly, it should be read in conjunction with papers presented by Sir Patrick Mayhew on 9 September and by the Irish government on 29

September. Both seemed to owe much to the SDLP analysis. The British discussion paper spoke of north–south institutions, of an 'agreed Ireland' and of establishing an Irish government office in the north and a Northern Ireland office in Dublin. That was enough for one SDLP member: 'It proves that the British government really is neutral about the north' – words that were to have a certain resonance when SF came into the picture. A *Newsletter* editorial (14 September 1992) described it as 'as lethal as an IRA semtex bomb'. Following a complaint that the government had not been 'robust' enough in defending the Union the paper was withdrawn. The Irish government paper accepted the idea of a six-member Commission, and of new institutions of government which should 'reflect both the democratic preferences of the electorate in Northern Ireland and the key external relationships . . . no purely internal structure can hope to cater adequately for the nationalist identity'.

The approach of the other three parties (Alliance, DUP and UUP) was minimalist in comparison. They sought (separately) an 85-member Assembly with powers akin to the 1974 model to be exercised through a series of committees which would reflect party strengths. They accepted too the notion of weighted majorities and an Assembly presided over by a Speaker. The UUP indicated later that it would be prepared to build on this by considering a Council of the British Isles and an inter-Irish relations committee, both of which would be consultative. They could not usurp the role of any new Assembly, nor would Dublin be permitted any executive responsibility.

By mid-summer several trends had revealed themselves. One was that the Dublin and London governments seemed to be acting in harmony. They were happy enough to postpone a putative Conference set for 27 July until 'not before September 28th' to allow for a smooth resumption of talks after the summer recess. A second was that the Irish government delegation composed of members of the Fianna Fail / Progressive Democrats coalition did not always speak with the same voice. A third was the degree to which the unionist parties were in disagreement about how to proceed after Strand 1. It began with a DUP walkout on 9 September from the constitutional talks subcommittee protesting that Articles 2 and 3 or the Irish constitution should have been at the head of the agenda rather than the fourth item. They did not return until 30 September but left two delegates as 'observers'. Meanwhile the UUP had participated in talks at Dublin Castle on 21 September and relations with the DUP suffered accordingly. Fourth, by October the talks had moved beyond generalities and become more specific and hence more difficult. The *Irish Times* (1 October 1992) captured the mood of pessimism: 'After five months, Strand 1 is deadlocked, and Strand 2 is moving desperately slowly. There is no public outpouring of good will and trust between the participants as such.'

Thereafter the talks went into decline but, notwithstanding that, the secretary of state gave an upbeat report to the Commons on 11 November when he said that the objectives of the talks process remained valid and achievable. In fact a more realistic summary was provided by Mark Brennock in the *Irish Times* on the same day when he wrote that what was 'initially a search for a historic new agreement became a search for heads of agreement, for elements of agreement, for a "soft landing" to allow an early resumption of talks and, finally, for an agreed statement'. But even that provided several negatives: 'The talks have not resulted in a comprehensive accommodation . . . objectives have not yet been achieved . . . no basis to agree a settlement . . . all regret that their efforts have not been blessed by greater agreement'.

The talks had opened in a climate of despair following another wave of violence. They had opened, too, against continuing SF concerns about 'marginalization'. By the time the talks had finished a few more political realities were imposing themselves. Loyalists were demonstrating yet again their capacity for sustained violence in which they could outmatch the IRA. A second was the election of Bill Clinton as American President: a Democrat in the White House held out the potential for an interventionist US role. A third was that Sir Patrick Mayhew sent out a coded message to the wider nationalist community in a speech at the

University of Ulster in December 1992. He acknowledged past British wrongs and paid obeisance to the historic figures of constitutional nationalism, contrasting them with Sinn Fein which had excluded itself from the talks: 'if its cause does have serious political purpose, then let it renounce unequivocally the use and threat of violence and demonstrate over a sufficient period that its renunciation is for real' – an unerring precursor of the Joint Declaration.

Towards the Joint Declaration

A word which recurs frequently in the earlier part of this chapter is 'process'. It is not unknown in the English language but was not part of political discourse in Northern Ireland. There politics has been a zero-sum game with all the spoils going to the victors with a huge dose of fatalism and frustration residing with the vanquished. Political activity, then, never was about negotiation and the skills which went with them until, that is, the post-Agreement period. It is possible to examine political life in Northern Ireland since about 1986 as a massive teach-in and crash course on the opportunities and constraints offered by politics. We have seen the painfully slow progress that has been made among the constitutional parties. Often it seemed to have as much validity as two bald men fighting over a comb and rarely did it rise above the level of megaphone diplomacy. So much of what has happened since 1986 has stressed the limitations on political manoeuvre and contrasts sharply with what appeared to unionists to have been a golden age when they were in control of Stormont. The new reality has stressed *their* marginality not only in relation to Irish nationalists but to their minority status inside the UK. Events since the signing of the Agreement suggest that for the first time in their history they have not been able to undo what they consider to be an act of British perfidy and that the politics of procrastination may have run its course.

If the unionist community detects a new assymetry illustrated by their powerlessness, Sinn Fein has also seen a marked decline in its fortunes since the heady days of the hunger strikes when it was able to marshal tens of thousands of people on to the streets and then convert that emotional outlet into electoral support. In that respect we must bear in mind that SF contests elections the length and breadth of Ireland. Hence while it could rely on a hard core 10 per cent vote in Northern Ireland it was winning less than 2 per cent in the Republic – hardly a mandate for a party which claimed to speak on behalf of all the people of Ireland. But it will be argued that the republicans built on adversity and began to look at the political process for opportunities rather than constraints. In doing so they had to contemplate ditching much of their historical baggage.

That was not going to be easy. Here was a movement which spoke with moral certitude on the inevitability of Irish unity; which had its own sense of 'history' fuelled by a mixture of manifest destiny – God had made Ireland an island and it was only natural that it should be reunited; and with a psychology of 'victimhood' – what Robert Elias (*The Politics of Victimisation* New York, Oxford University Press, 1986, p. 233) calls 'the political economy of helplessness'.

Irish republicans believed that they had been engaged in a long and just campaign, a war of attrition which would eventually wear down British resistance to remaining in Northern Ireland. They traced their roots back, if not to Wolfe Tone and the 1798 rebellion, then certainly to the 1916 rising. They were hyperconscious of that pantheon of martyred republicans from Tone to the men of 1916 – and in this present generation all those who had given their lives (including the hunger strikers) for the cause of Irish freedom. Conveniently that enabled them to forget their own misdemeanours so that they were able to project themselves as defenders of their own community and of the sacred torch of Irish freedom. Theirs was a politics of sacrifice driven by the fact that they could not forget their fallen comrades. Nothing less than unadulterated Irish freedom would compensate for their sacrifice.

This was a mindset which was oblivious to the Protestant sense of victimhood and which had a fundamental distrust of *all* conventional politics. If proof were needed all one need read is a statement from the political prisoners following the end of the hunger strikes in October 1981. The very long statement is couched in religious sentiment in that it presents a cast of mind which prizes the 'moral against the actual and the bearing of witness as against success' (O. MacDonagh, *States of Mind*, London, Allen and Unwin, 1983, p. 13). Much of its venom was directed at those inside its own community such as the catholic hierarchy, the SDLP and the parties in Dail Eireann. The SDLP, for example, were 'devoid of principle, direction and courage . . . Their whole leadership combined do not possess a fraction of the moral fibre demonstrated so valiantly by our comrades':

> Our comrades have lit with their very lives an eternal beacon which will inspire this nation and people to rise and crush oppression forever, and this nation can be proud that it produced such a quality of manhood. (*Irish Times*, 5 October 1981)

Here was language in the heroic style and here was a message which could have been lifted out of the 1916 Proclamation. Any one who wanted to alter this mindset had to be conscious of republican iconography and symbolism. Change would have to come from within.

But there needed to be signs on the larger political horizon to encourage reformers within the republican movement. We have referred to some of those changes above: the hostile impact of the Anglo-Irish Agreement on IRA resistance; greater political sensitivity by the authorities to republican fears as shown in some of the speeches of Peter Brooke; and the talks process which encompassed the 'totality of relationships'. There was also movement at grassroots level. Some of it was 'accidental' – the tactic of electoralism following the emotional upsurge of the hunger strike – but some of it was carefully contrived: the decision taken at the 1986 Sinn Fein Ard Fheis to take any seats it won at Dail elections. The symbolic significance of this decision went largely unnoticed. In effect it was the first recognition of any Irish parliamentary assembly by Sinn Fein since partition, and it enjoyed the unanimous endorsement of the IRA Army Council. An inevitable split ensued but the breakaway group, Republican Sinn Fein, was of little political or military consequence.

All of this has to be set against the IRA's continuing war. We have noted the devastating effect of the Brighton bomb at the Conservative Party Conference in 1984 which killed five people including a Conservative MP. The IRA's statement of admission was simplicity itself:

> The IRA claims responsibility for the detonation of 100 lb of gelignite in Brighton against the British Cabinet and Tory warmongers. Mrs Thatcher will now realise that Britain cannot occupy our country and torture our prisoners and shoot our people on their own streets and get away with it. Today we were unlucky, but remember we only have to be lucky once – you will have to be lucky always. Give Ireland peace and there will be no war.

By this simple act the IRA was sending a message that violence could have substantial political consequences – hence the upbeat note in their statement. But contrast that with another incident, the bomb which went off in Enniskillen on Remembrance Sunday in November 1987. It killed eleven bystanders commemorating their dead from two world wars. That single incident did untold damage to the republican strategy of the armalite and the ballot box: indeed at the next local council elections Sinn Fein lost four of its eight seats in Fermanagh, the site of the bomb. It has to be seen, too, in conjunction with many other 'mistakes' for which the IRA was guilty, for example targetting the wrong people. Nor did it escape their notice that there had been a resurgence in Loyalist violence, much of it directed at their own members. This, and more, called into question the efficacy of the armed struggle and was another reason to reassess the nature of the campaign.

That reassessment had begun as early as 1986. Sinn Fein

had not been invited to participate in the New Ireland Forum of 1983–4. At the very least their absence highlighted their marginality inside the nationalist community on the island. In any case the younger northern leadership had begun to evaluate the place for republicanism after so many years of conflict. Their support was more rooted in their community than that of their predecessors: 'the circumstances which shaped the support for the IRA are above all the experience of the barricade days from 1969–72. These days are of continuing importance not just in terms of the IRA but because they saw the development of tremendous communal solidarity, more than a memory of which remains today' (G. Adams, *The Politics of Irish Freedom*, Brandon, 1986, p. 52). The present-day IRA was rooted deeply in the communities which had thrown up the barricades in 1969. It sought and, for the most part, gained legitimacy in those areas. In that respect it was unlike other guerrilla movements which arose in western Europe (such as the Red Brigade or the Baader-Meinhof gang) about this time. It was *in* and *of* its community. It could not operate successfully without the tacit support of the people it claimed to represent.

But there were those such as Gerry Adams who were concerned with more than simply continuing the sacrificial struggle of his predecessors. It had to have a wider *political* meaning: 'In the past the republican movement was a separatist movement with radical tendencies. In its current embodiment the radical tendency is for the first time in control' (*ibid.*, p. 162). We have noted that the power of the radical element began to grow after the 1975 ceasefire which had had such a detrimental effect on the IRA war machine. A younger, northern leadership led by people like Gerry Adams and Martin McGuinness began to change direction to the armalite *and* the ballot box, especially after the 'success' of the hunger strike. But that, again as we have seen, had its downside – hence the shift towards the peace process. And if one had to highlight the landmarks which led republicans to accepting the Joint Declaration one would mention *The Politics of Irish Freedom*, Adams' political manifesto published as early as 1986; the SDLP–Sinn Fein dialogue conducted during 1988 (and other talks which Sinn Fein had with protestant clergy); *Towards A Strategy For Peace*, a 1988 Sinn Fein document; coded messages sent by the British government and then secret contacts between government and individuals such as Martin McGuinness which ran between October 1990 and November 1993; and finally the dialogue from 1988 onwards between John Hume and Gerry Adams.

We have alluded already to the Adams's manifesto but it should be seen in conjunction with the Sinn Fein decision taken in 1986 to abandon its abstentionist policy towards the Dail. We need not detain ourselves unduly with the Sinn Fein policy document of 1988 except to underline its naivity when it stated that the 'establishment of a society free from British interference, with the Union at an end, will see sectarianism shrivel and with the emergence of class politics a re-alignment of political forces along left and right lines. The Irish democracy thus created will usher in the conditions for a permanent peace, a demilitarisation of the situation, and the creation of a just society'. That document appeared in March, the same month in which John Hume established contact with Sinn Fein. The timing probably was not accidental. In the wake of the Enniskillen bomb Hume may have decided that it was the right psychological moment to challenge the armed struggle.

In a letter to Gerry Adams on St Patrick's Day 1988 Hume claimed that the IRA's campaign was doing more damage to the people it claimed to be protecting; that it was simplistic to state that 'the cause of all the violence is the British presence in Ireland'; that it is the people, rather than territory, of Ireland who have to be united; and that the IRA 'methods and their strategy have actually become more sacred than their cause'. Here he quoted (tellingly) Wolfe Tone, the secular (and protestant) saint of Irish republicanism, on the distinction between objectives and means. There followed a series of meetings between the two sides which culminated in September 1988 when the gap between them was too broad to be bridged, although they did say that they would continue to meet in public and in private as the opportunity arose.

The process highlighted several features. For the first time Sinn Fein policies were being scrutinized closely by a party which sought the same end of Irish unity – and during the dialogue the SDLP emerged as the *republican* party and Sinn Fein as the *nationalist* one. It was the SDLP which invoked the ghosts of the republican past and reminded Sinn Fein that Tone and Pearse had called off the armed struggle rather than commit their people to further bloodshed. Second, the dialogue may have moved the debate away from moral certitude. Third, the dialogue rehearsed many of the issues which appeared in the Joint Declaration: for example, the SDLP suggested a 'Forum for Peace and Reconciliation'; the SDLP's blunt assertion that Britain no longer had any strategic or economic interest for remaining in Ireland; and finally the debate about self-determination was removed from its theological plinth and placed in the harsh political world of the late twentieth century.

Much of this realism was reflected in *Towards A Lasting Peace In Ireland*, published by Sinn Fein in February 1992. It recognized that unionist fears would have to be addressed and that British withdrawal could be accomplished only through cooperation with both governments in consultation with the Northern Ireland parties. This represented considerable SF movement because now it recognized the legitimacy and role of the Irish government as well as the rights of northern protestants. Finally Sinn Fein raised its eyes above the parapet by taking account of the international dimension and the political implications of European Union.

Public contact with the SDLP was not renewed until April 1993 in the Hume / Adams dialogue. Now Sinn Fein was in search of a new political role. The 'Long War' had reached a state of military stasis and the IRA was admitting to more 'accidents' at the same time as loyalists were targetting SF members – in just over a year they killed thirteen. In addition a Fianna Fail / Labour coalition returned to office in Dublin in January 1993 was giving Northern Ireland a very high priority. The 'Programme for Partnership Government' stated that it 'would mobilize all the resources of the Government which can contribute to this process [and which was working towards] an accommodation of the two traditions in Ireland based on the principle that both must have equally satisfactory, secure and durable, political, administrative and symbolic expression as set out in the Forum Report'.

Contrast this with a joint statement issued after the first Hume / Adams meeting which read, initially, like a stale reiteration of Irish nationalism. They spoke of the futility of an internal settlement and insisted that the 'Irish people as a whole have a right to national self-determination'. But the statement was more subtle than that and recognized that any 'new agreement is only achievable and viable if it can earn and enjoy the allegiance of the different traditions of this island by accommodating diversity and providing for national reconciliation'. The Hume / Adams talks were suspended on 25 September 1993 to enable the Irish government to consider their joint paper, the broad principles of which '[would] be for wider consideration between the two governments'.

One of the purposes of wider consideration was to allow the governments to keep their distance from Sinn Fein and seek to assuage unionist fears. Towards this end the Tanaiste, Dick Spring, set out on 27 October six democratic principles for a sustainable peace which were meant to complement John Hume's efforts. They were: the people of Ireland, north and south, should freely determine their future; this could be expressed in new structures arising out of the three-stranded relationship; there could be no change in Northern Ireland's status without freely-given majority consent; this could be withheld (a point amended later to keep the statement in line with the majority consent principle of Art. 1 of the Anglo-Irish Agreement); the consent principles would be written into the Irish constitution; a place would be found at the negotiation table for SF once the IRA had renounced violence.

The Joint Declaration

All of this was written into the Joint Declaration signed by the British and Irish prime ministers at Downing Street on 15 December 1993. The declaration was the outcome of all the subterranean political movement we have described above. Unlike the Anglo-Irish Agreement which was about process and structure this was about principles and the building blocks on which peace could be constructed. One of the more astute commentaries on it came from Sir David Goodall a former High Commissioner to India and, more importantly, one of the chief architects of the 1985 Agreement. He understood the nuances, actors and dynamics involved in this particular conflict. He noted the skilful drafting and abundant use of coded language which have 'laid a veneer of unanimity over what are still divergent and in some respects directly conflicting interests'. Hence it is 'a minor diplomatic masterpiece . . . [which] is not a formal agreement or treaty setting the framework for a comprehensive constitutional settlement; it is a political statement of attitude and intent directed primarily at the IRA. The two heads of government have carefully shelved all the difficult longer term issues . . . in order to make a bid for an IRA ceasefire' (Goodall, 'Terrorists on the Spot', *The Tablet*, 25 December 1993/1 January 1994, p. 1676). It might also be said that a bid was made to woo loyalist paramilitaries, especially in para. 5 where civil rights and religious liberties were enunciated.

Although it is a complex document and a piece of tortuous syntax, Goodall provided a neat precis of the declaration:

> So the central thrust of the declaration lies in the British Government's assurance that 'they have no selfish strategic or economic interest in Northern Ireland'; in the Irish Government's stress on the reality of the unionist veto; in the (significantly differentiated) commitments of the two governments to self-determination for the people of Ireland; and in the offer of a place at the negotiating table for Sinn Fein once violence has been brought to an end and definitively renounced. All else is top dressing . . .

Events since the signing of the declaration indicate how sensitive a plant it is. It has received bi-partisan support in both the British and Irish parliaments but the DUP remains hostile and elements in the UUP have been lukewarm. There has been considerable international support, in particular from the US administration and the EU.

The republican movement has edged its way very cautiously towards acceptance. The IRA did not announce its 'total cessation of military operations' until midnight August 31 1994. It refused to use the word 'permanent' and it did not accept the Downing Street Declaration as a solution: 'A solution will only be found as a result of inclusive negotiations. Others, not least the British Government, have a duty to face up to their responsibilities.' Government had insisted that the Declaration was a free-standing document which needed no further clarification. SF demurred. It argued that there were too many ambiguities and that, in any case, as a democratic organization it needed to conduct a series of consultations with its supporters on the ground. In the meantime the Irish government acted as a conduit offering whatever clarification it could and by serving as a line of communication to Mr Major. In the end it was the British government which blinked first by responding in May 1995 to twenty questions posed by Sinn Fein passed on to it by the Taoiseach. The government acknowledged that parties were not obliged to accept the Declaration – simply to declare and demonstrate a permanent end to violence and to abide by the democratic process. Further it accepted the validity of Sinn Fein's electoral mandate and that 'no political objective could properly be excluded from discussion in the talks process'. While this represented a victory of sorts for republicans we should remember that by using the Dublin government as a conduit Sinn Fein and the IRA were recognizing its legitimacy.

Other means were being found to keep republicans inside the democratic process. The first was to be found within paragraph 11 of the Declaration in which the Irish government signalled its intention to establish a Forum for Peace and Reconciliation 'to make recommendations on ways in which agreement and trust between both traditions in Ireland can be promoted and established'. From its inaugural meeting on 28 October 1994 Sinn Fein participated as a fully-fledged member. The Forum met on a weekly basis and as business proceeded its emphasis shifted from considering options for a united Ireland to being more concerned with the principle of consent through a process which 'could most contribute to creating a new era of trust and co-operation on this island'. The potential of this exercise should not be underestimated. It has enabled Sinn Fein to move beyond the marginalized and become another party in the democratic debate. In turn this has meant that Sinn Fein has had to operate under normal constraints imposed by the realities of competing party claims where there is little room for millenarian rhetoric. Earlier (19 January 1994) the Irish government lifted its broadcasting ban on republicans; Mr Major followed suit on 16 September. Other manifestations were a symbolic handshake between the Taoiseach, Albert Reynolds, John Hume and Gerry Adams on 6 September; and an announcement in November from the Minister of Justice of the early release of IRA prisoners from the Republic's jails.

The Clinton administration played an important role by granting Gerry Adams a 48-hour visa to visit the US in February 1994 to explain the Sinn Fein position but this decision was taken against the advice of the British government, the State Department and prominent Irish-Americans such as House Speaker, Tom Foley. When Adams demonstrated that he was not a Nelson Mandela there was a feeling that the jeremiahs had been proved correct. In fact the US trip may have had a sobering effect on Sinn Fein because now it realized that it had to address the concerns of the wider community. Two further visas during 1994 symbolized the growing international legitimacy of Sinn Fein. These culminated in a meeting and a handshake between Adams and President Clinton in the White House on St Patrick's Day 1995.

All of this has to be set against the continuing violence until the IRA announcement of 31 August. Already there had been 60 fatalities arising from the violence and there had been several false dawns. The Sinn Fein Ard-Fheis had been smothered in a fog of rhetoric in February; the IRA had declared only a three-day cease-fire over the Easter period when many had been waiting for a historic announcement; and at a long-awaited national delegate conference in County Donegal the message which emerged was blurred and obfuscatory so that the exercise became a public relations disaster for Sinn Fein. Lessons were learned and resulted in an announcement from the IRA on 31 August 1994: 'Recognizing the potential of the current situation and in order to enhance the democratic peace process, the IRA will call a ceasefire from midnight Wednesday, August 31. It will be a complete cessation of military operations and all units have been instructed accordingly.'

While it refused to use the word 'permanent' in relation to the cessation of violence it was enough to enable the British prime minister to arrive at a working assumption that violence had ended for good; and three months, almost to the day, after 31 August a Sinn Fein delegation sat down with British officials to engage in preliminary, exploratory dialogue. That dialogue has not always been smooth so that by the middle of 1995 a serious rift had occurred on the issue of decommissioning of IRA weapons. Sinn Fein wanted it to be discussed against the broader backcloth of the decommissioning of *all* weapons and argued that what really counted was the absence of violence. There was nothing in its previous history to suggest that it would unilaterally hand over its weapons. Government needed a firmer assurance than that if only to keep mainstream unionists on board. A stalemate ensued but, at the time of writing, jaw jaw was still in operation.

Loyalists did not reciprocate in like manner immediately. There was a suspicion that a secret deal had been done between the government and republicans. In any case, unionists noted, huge caches of weapons remained in the hands of the IRA and a 'permanent' cessation had not been announced. This was reflected in an announcement from the CLMC (Combined Loyalist Military Command) on 13 October 1994 that it would 'unilaterally cease all operational hostilities [although the] permanence of our ceasefire will be completely dependent upon the continued cessation of all nationalist / republican violence, the sole responsibility for a return to War lies with them'. In a statement which boded well for the peace process the CLMC offered 'the loved ones of all innocent victims over the past twenty-five years, abject and true remorse'. So, one cease-fire was dependent on the other, and both were predicated on potentially conflicting analyses of the situation – the IRA believed 'we are entering a new situation, a new opportunity', whereas the CLMC stated bluntly: 'The Union is safe'. Despite this the absence of violence was creating the conditions for an inclusive dialogue to begin.

Both governments responded to this with the publication of the Framework documents on 22 February 1995. The emphasis was firmly on the plural because they were concerned with the totality of relationships *and* with arrangements for devolved structures for Northern Ireland. The papers were complex and wordy and deliberately ambiguous because they had to offer something for every one. The subtitle of the 'external' document, *A New Framework For Agreement*, was significant because it referred to a 'shared understanding . . . to assist discussion and negotiation involving the Northern Ireland parties'. In other words it was not a blueprint nor was it meant to be a grand pronouncement *de haut en bas*. It was about process and inclusivity and it included elements of virtually every policy document of the past five years. It was meant to ensure that all parties stayed at the negotiating table. The Unionist parties expressed deep reservations but knew that they could bring their own suggestions to that table.

Notwithstanding this understandable reaction we should not ignore the huge potential contained within the peace process. All recognized now fragile was the process. The killings may have stopped but paramilitary punishment beatings continued. Leaders like Adams were aware that they might get too far ahead of the rank and file. Their communities were anxious that the political prisoners be released at the earliest possible moment. Public opinion seemed anxious to give peace a chance: in the one Westminster by-election since the publication of the Framework documents, that in North Down on 15 June 1995 the successful candidate was a 'United Kingdom Unionist', Robert McCartney.

He had fought his campaign as a referendum against the peace process yet the turnout was less than 40 per cent, the lowest in Northern Ireland's electoral history. It was hardly a ringing endorsement more a sign in a strongly unionist constituency that people remained sceptical. That was in sharp contrast to the deep bitterness which had accompanied the Anglo-Irish Agreement of 1985.

Governments and seasoned commentators were convinced that this was 'for real'. Now was the time to construct an audit for the peace dividend and one for the deficit – for example, what was to happen the whole security apparatus? Just as tellingly the dynamics of peace raised several major issues: if peace could be envisaged, could people begin to think positively and audaciously? Could they overcome a culture of fatalism and despair? Would there be political realignments? What role would forgiveness and redemption have to play? Would a market economy replace the politics of economic dependency? Is there a place for a new vocabulary and political discourse based on the realities of the collapse of the old world order and the rise of postnationalism? Can we think beyond (to quote the Polish Nobel Laureate, Czeslaw Milosz) 'the memory of wounds'?

9 Conclusion

There are simple solutions to the problem of Northern Ireland, such as 'Brits outs', full integration in the United Kingdom or independence, with or without repartition, but these are only for the simple-minded. 'Brits outs' begs the question of who exactly the 'Brits' are: does this group merely comprise members of the administration and security forces who were recruited in Great Britain, or does it include all those who still see themselves as 'British'? This latter group might include over a million people; more than one-fifth of the population of the island. Even the Provisionals recognize that there would have to be a phased dismantling of the links with the rest of the United Kingdom, and most plans which aim at the 'reunification' of Ireland assume a continuance of the British subvention for some years. Unionists regard 'Brits out' as a deeply insulting proposal since they believe that their rights to live in Ireland and to remain within the United Kingdom are as well-founded as those of any nationalist. Indeed, they might argue that it was extreme nationalists who partitioned Ireland in the first place by seceding from the UK. If 'Brits out' refers only to the British army (with or without its Irish soldiers) and implies also the dismantling of the RUC, then it is likely that renewed large-scale sectarian violence would ensue.

Throughout the Troubles the level of loyalist-inspired violence was on the whole restricted by the fact that however unhappy the protestant community may have been with the specifics of British political and security policy, their basic requirement – the maintenance of the Union – was still being met by London, and was guaranteed, so long as a majority of the population approve, by both the British and Irish governments. Many protestants loyally serve in the police and the UDR/RIR, but if the British government were unilaterally to abandon Northern Ireland many of these people might be prepared to defend their community and their status by armed force. The restraints on violence which are provided by the presence of the British army, moreover, would be removed and the way could be open to a bloodbath.

This would also be a route towards 'independence'. Some loyalists have contemplated independence as the only honourable course. It is difficult to see how this option could ever be taken seriously except *in extremis*. Northern Ireland is so small and so economically disadvantaged that living standards would drop catastrophically if it became independent, unless, of course, London was prepared to continue its subvention. It has been suggested that a measure of repartition might ease some of the province's communal problems, but no amount of tinkering about with the border can help the 100,000 or so catholics in Belfast who would inevitably remain inside Northern Ireland.

Full integration with the rest of the United Kingdom has latterly become a widely-canvassed option. The 'Campaign for Equal Citizenship' which backed Robert McCartney's attempt to win a Westminster seat in June 1987 on a 'Real Unionist' ticket argued that the only way to take the border out of politics was to establish Northern Ireland firmly and permanently as an integral part of the United Kingdom and to put aside any notions that the province might ever become part of an independent Ireland. The campaign never really gained very much momentum, though in 1989 the British Conservative party were persuaded to organize in the province and enjoyed modest success in the local government elections that year. A small group, the 'Friends of the Union', formed in 1986, continues to press the integrationist case. The Labour Party refuses to allow people in Northern Ireland to join and is in any case officially committed to the idea of a united Ireland by consent. Many British Conservatives have long since ceased to view Ulster Unionists as natural allies, a change of mind to which Ulstermen themselves have powerfully contributed. The unedifying spectacle of loyalist leaders physically attacking the Secretary of State for Northern Ireland – as happened after the Anglo-Irish Agreement – or of MPs such as Ian Paisley accusing Ministers of the Crown of being 'traitors' is only likely to confirm British political activists in the wisdom of keeping Northern Ireland at arm's length.

British policy towards Northern Ireland since 1921 has in effect been designed with precisely that end in mind. The whole point of Lloyd George's Irish settlement – the establishment of the Irish Free State (now the Republic) and Northern Ireland – was to take the Irish question out of British politics, which it had bedevilled for more than fifty years. This policy succeeded until 1968–9 when the violence in the province once more thrust Irish politics on to the British political agenda. The consistent policy of each British administration since direct rule was imposed in 1972 has been to create some form of powersharing devolved administration. A devolved government will help take Irish affairs off the British agenda, and powersharing might ensure that it stays that way in the long term. This policy, however, has so far failed. The 1974 executive which came closest to succeeding collapsed in the face of powerful loyalist opposition and apparent British indifference. The subsequent inability of the province's political leaders to agree on any other arrangement has led London to the view that Dublin might have a tangible role to play in the Northern Ireland political process: hence the Anglo-Irish Agreement, the Downing Street Declaration and the Framework Documents, which formally provide such a role and also embody London's continuing faith in a powersharing solution. Although loyalist reaction to the Agreement was undoubtedly much more vigorous than had been expected, the less militant response to the subsequent developments has raised hopes that some agreement might be secured among the Northern Ireland political parties.

In the meantime London most persevere with direct rule, which successive opinion polls have shown is the least unacceptable political option. Although Northern Ireland continues to be a political nuisance to the United Kingdom, its retention is not so very costly in global terms. The cost of the Northern Ireland subvention to the British Exchequer, although great, is by no means unbearable. The corrosive impact of Northern Ireland's recent history has made it very difficult indeed to envisage long-term political harmony. Yet the ending of the killings (though not that of violence) since the cease-fires has provided a much-needed and welcomed opportunity for the communities to inch towards some sort of political consensus. But the process will require patience, dedication and a willingness more to seek out areas of common ground than to assert already all-to-well demarcated points of difference.

Since the problem is complex, the 'solution' must be so too. The development of new political structures, such as are envisaged in the 1995 Framework Documents, can only provide part of the answer. Such structures in any case are more likely to reflect changing communal attitudes than actually alter them. The government – any government – must provide means by which law and order can acceptably be maintained within the province. The process by which the RUC has become more acceptable to the minority community must be continued and every effort must be made to ensure that all the security forces act in an impartial a fashion as possible. The current government is also well aware that Northern Ireland's continuing economic and social disadvantage contribute towards communal tensions. But the problem here is circular. While high levels of unemployment may increase the likelihood of violence, continued unrest will in turn inhibit new investment. Different administrations at different times have placed the main emphasis on particular aspects of the Northern Ireland problem – political, security or socio-economic – but the fact remains that no one strand can be wholly isolated and that to succeed any policy must take into account the interrelationships between each aspect. Over the years it seems that this is one lesson which has been learned by the administration of Northern Ireland.

The 'Troubles' which we have been discussing are deep-seated indeed, and any resolution of the conflict will only take place over a very long period. It is all too easy to lapse into a helpless pessimism when contemplating the problem and surely even Sisyphus had an easy time of it compared to those concerned with the province's future. In 1995 four main actors remain on the political stage: Northern Ireland's two communities and the two sovereign governments. London and Dublin have agreed on a framework for progress and this has the support of a majority of the catholics. The loyalists, however, are still out in the cold. But there appears to be a slow unionist realization that old methods and old clichés are no longer relevant. In short, recent developments have at least encouraged that psychological breakthrough and in constitutional terms have challenged the rigid concepts of state sovereignty and 'national self-determination' – on both sides – which have blocked political progress in the province. This process, if it continues, might give Northern Ireland its best chance since 1974 of moving towards some sort of acceptable internal accommodation.

Appendix

Deaths Caused by the Violence in Northern Ireland, 1969–1994

Year	RUC	Regular army	UDR/ RIR	Civilians	Total
1969	1	–	–	12	13
1970	2	–	–	23	25
1971	11	43	5	115	174
1972	17	103	26	321	467
1973	13	58	8	171	250
1974	15	28	7	166	216
1975	11	14	6	216	247
1976	23	14	15	245	297
1977	14	15	14	69	112
1978	10	14	7	50	81
1979	14	38	10	51	113
1980	9	8	9	50	76
1981	21	10	13	57	101
1982	12	21	7	57	97
1983	18	5	10	44	77
1984	8	9	10	37	64
1985	23	2	4	25	54
1986	12	4	8	37	61
1987	16	3	8	66	93
1988	6	21	12	54	93
1989	9	12	2	39	62
1990	12	7	8	49	76
1991	6	5	8	75	94
1992	3	3	3	76	85
1993	6	6	2	70	84
1994	3	1	2	54	60

Outline Chronology

1912–14 Home Rule crisis: formation of unionist Ulster Volunteer Force and nationalist Irish Volunteers; passage of Home Rule Act, but operation postponed by outbreak of First World War.

1916 Easter Rising in Dublin.

1919–21 Anglo-Irish war, during which Ireland was partitioned into Northern Ireland and what became known as the Irish Free State following the Anglo-Irish Treaty of December 1921.

1937 New constitution promulgated in Dublin asserting jurisdiction over the whole island of Ireland.

1949 Irish Republic established. Westminster passed Ireland Act affirming that a change in the constitutional status of the North could only occur with the consent of the Northern Ireland parliament.

1956–62 Sporadic IRA campaign along the Border.

1963 Terence O'Neill became prime minister of Northern Ireland and began modest series of reforms.

1968 Civil rights campaign began in summer, continuing with marches and demonstrations to end of year.

1969 Rioting in Londonderry and Belfast during August; army deployed on peacekeeping duties. Provisionals (PIRA) broke away from official IRA.

1970 Ulster Defence Regiment inaugurated to replace 'B' Specials; SDLP formed.

1971   First soldier killed by PIRA; internment without trial began, followed by widespread rioting.

1972   Thirteen men shot dead by army in Londonderry (Bloody Sunday) on 30 January; UK Embassy in Dublin subsequently burnt down. N. Ireland government resigned after Heath announced transfer of law and order to Westminster. Direct rule established. Nine killed and 130 injured by 19 PIRA bombs in Belfast (Bloody Friday) on 21 July.

1973   Sunningdale conference marked establishment of power-sharing: British, Irish and Northern Irish representatives affirmed that constitutional status of Northern Ireland could only be changed by consent of Protestant majority and agreed to set up a Council of Ireland.

1974   Power-sharing executive of Faulkner (Chief Executive) unionists, SDLP and Alliance formally took office. In May UWC strike caused Executive to collapse.

1975   Phasing out of internment.

1976   Widely supported 'Peace People' demonstrations raised hopes of community reconciliation, but proved to be only a temporary emotional expression of frustration at continuing violence.

1977   'Ulsterisation' policy introduced; abortive Loyalist strike protesting against security policy.

1978   Republican prisoners at Maze prison launched 'dirty protest' in support of better prison conditions.

1979   Conservative Northern Ireland spokesman Airey Neave murdered by INLA bomb at House of Commons. PIRA bombers killed 18 soldiers near Warrenpoint, Co. Down, and assassinated Lord Mountbatten near his holiday home in the Republic.

1980   Mrs Thatcher and Charles Haughey (Irish Prime Minister) reached agreement on 'new and closer political co-operation'. Republican prisoners in H-blocks of Maze Prison began 'fast unto death' in support of 'political status', but call off protest at New Year.

1981   Bobby Sands began new hunger strike campaign and was followed at regular intervals by further hunger strikers. Sands died on 66th day. 9 further hunger strikers died between May and Aug before campaign was called off.

1982   Provisional Sinn Fein polled 10% of votes in N. Ireland Assembly elections.

1983   Fourteen UVF men jailed after first 'supergrass' trial. Just before Christmas PIRA car bomb at Harrods store in London killed 5 and injured 80.

1984   New Ireland Forum Report recommended unity by consent. President Reagan in Dublin condemned the use of violence in Northern Ireland. Bomb at Grand Hotel Brighton during Conservative Party Conference killed 5 people.

1985   RUC and Protestant demonstrators clashed violently over re-routing of traditional parades away from Catholic areas. PIRA campaign against businessmen who trade with the security forces. Anglo-Irish Agreement signed on 15 November by British and Irish prime ministers at Hillsborough Castle, county Down; massive loyalist demonstrations against Agreement follow.

1986   Unionists lost one seat to SDLP in 15 by-elections caused by their mass resignation from the House of Commons in protest against the Agreement. SDLP took votes from Provisional candidates. Loyalist campaign against Agreement marked by non-co-operation in local government, marches, heightened paramilitary activity and attacks on off-duty RUC personnel and their families. Northern Ireland Assembly wound up.

1987   Charles Haughey, leader of Fianna Fail, forms government in Dublin after general election in which Sinn Fein won less than 2% of vote. 12 people died in internal INLA feud which began at the end of 1986; 8 PIRA men were killed during attack on police station at Loughgall, county Armagh. Remembrance

Sunday bomb at Enniskillen kills eleven.

1988   John Hume and Gerry Adams meet for talks. PIRA campaign against British servicemen in Europe; 3 PIRA volunteers shot dead in Gibraltar.

1989   PIRA bomb kills 10 military bandsmen in Deal, Kent. Stevens inquiry finds some collusion between security forces and loyalist paramilitaries.

1990   Secretary of State Peter Brooke launches three-stranded talks initiative. John Major replaces Margaret Thatcher as British prime minister. PIRA call 3-day Christmas cease-fire.

1991   PIRA mortar-bomb 10 Downing Street. Brooke holds bilateral meetings with DUP, UUP, Alliance and SDLP, but general talks do not advance beyond the preliminary stage. PIRA Christmas ceasefire becomes an annual event.

1992   Five catholics murdered by loyalist gunmen at a book-makers in Lower Ormeau, Belfast. Sinn Fein lose West Belfast seat to SDLP in Westminster general election. UDR and Royal Irish Rangers amalgamated into the Royal Irish Regiment. Massive bomb outside the Baltic Exchange, City of London. PIRA campaign of car bombs against Belfast and provincial towns. UDA banned.

1993   PIRA bomb in Warrington kills two children; further attacks on City of London. PIRA bomb in Shankill Road fish shop kills 10; loyalists respond with 11 killings over five days. Hume–Adams contacts. Bill Clinton elected US president with Irish-American support. Downing Street Declaration (15 December) signed by John Major and Taoiseach Albert Reynolds commits British and Irish government to a joint approach to Northern Ireland.

1994   Gerry Adams granted visa to visit the USA. PIRA call three-day Easter ceasefire. Loyalist paramilitaries mount incendiary attacks in the Republic. UVF kill 6 catholics at Loughinisland, county Down. PIRA (31 August) and Combined Loyalist Military Command (13 October) declare ceasefires.

Fine Gael leader John Bruton succeeds Albert Reynolds as Taoiseach.

1995   Regular troops progressively withdrawn from active duties in Northern Ireland. Official British contacts begin with Sinn Fein. 'Framework Documents' published by British and Irish governments (22 February) outlining possible constitutional and administrative arrangements for the province.

Dramatis Personae

ADAMS, GERRY (b. 1949). Republican activist and Sinn Fein Westminster MP for West Belfast 1983–92.

ANNESLEY, SIR HUGH (b. 1939). RUC Chief Constable since 1989.

BRADFORD, REVEREND ROBERT (1941–81). Ulster Unionist MP for South Belfast assassinated by Provisional IRA in November 1981.

BROOKE, PETER (b. 1934). Conservative MP and Secretary of State for Northern Ireland 1989–92.

BRUTON, JOHN (b. 1947). Leader of Fine Gael from 1990 and Taoiseach (prime minister) of the Irish Republic from 1994.

CARSON, SIR EDWARD (1854–1935). Unionist MP 1892–1921 and leader of opposition to Irish home rule.

CHICHESTER-CLARK, JAMES (b. 1923). Leader of Ulster Unionist Party and Prime Minister of Northern Ireland 1969–71.

CRAIG, SIR JAMES (LORD CRAIGAVON) (1871–1940). Unionist leader and first prime minister of Northern Ireland 1921–40.

CRAIG, WILLIAM (b. 1924) Westminster MP at Stormont 1960–72 (cabinet minister 1962–8). Westminster MP 1974–9. Only leader of Vanguard Unionist Progressive Party 1973–8.

DE VALERA, EAMON (1882–1975). Veteran Irish republican leader. President of Irish Republic 1959–73.

FAULKNER, BRIAN (1921–77). Leader of Ulster Unionist Party and Prime Minister of Northern Ireland 1971–2. Chief Executive in powersharing administration in 1974. Leader of Unionist Party of Northern Ireland 1974–6.

FITT, GERARD (b. 1926). Westminster MP for West Belfast 19666–83. Leader of Social Democratic and Labour Party from its foundation in 1970 to 1979. Member of powersharing executive in 1974. Created Lord Fitt in 1983.

FITZGERALD, GARRET (b. 1926) Taoiseach (prime minister) of the Irish Republic 1981–March 1982 and December 1982–7. Leader of Fine Gael Party 1977–87.

HAUGHEY, CHARLES (b. 1925). Taoiseach (prime minister) of the Irish Republic 1979–81, 1982 and 1987–92. Leader of Fianna Fail party 1979–92.

HERMON, SIR JOHN (b. 1929). Chief Constable of the Royal Ulster Constabulary 1980–9.

HUME, JOHN (b. 1937). Westminster MP for Foyle since 1983. Leader of Social Democratic and Labour Party since 1979. Member of powersharing executive in 1974.

KING, TOM (b. 1933) Conservative MP and Secretary of State for Northern Ireland 1985–9.

LYNCH, JACK (b. 1917). Fianna Fail politicians and Taoiseach (prime minister) of the Irish Republic 1966–73 and 1977–9.

MACBRIDE, SEAN (1904–88). IRA leader in 1920s and 1930s. Cabinet minister in Dublin 1948–51. Winner of Nobel and Lenin Peace Prizes.

MCCUSKER, HAROLD (1940–90). Deputy leader of Ulster Unionist Party 1982–90 and Westminster MP for Armagh/Upper Bann 1974–90.

MCGUINNESS, MARTIN (b. 1950). Republican activist and Sinn Fein Northern Ireland Assembly member for Londonderry, 1982–6.

MACSTIOFAIN, SEAN (b. 1928). Chief of Staff of Provisional IRA 1970–2.

MAYHEW, SIR PATRICK (b. 1929). Conservative MP and Secretary of State for Northern Ireland from 1992.

MOLYNEAUX, JAMES (b. 1920). Westminster MP since 1970. Leader of Ulster Unionist Party 1979–95.

MORRISON, DANNY (b. 1953). Sinn Fein director of publicity and Northern Ireland Assembly member for Mid-Ulster 1982–6.

O'NEILL, TERENCE (1914–90). Leader of Ulster Unionist Party and Prime Minister of Northern Ireland, 1963–9.

OLDFIELD, SIR MAURICE (1915–80). Head of Secret Intelligence Service (MI6) 1965–77. Northern Ireland Security Co-ordinator 1979–90.

PAISLEY, REVEREND IAN (b. 1926). Moderator of Free Presbyterian Church. Found and leader of Democratic Unionist Party since 1971. Westminster MP for North Antrim from 1970.

POWELL, ENOCH (b. 1912). Conservative MP 1950–74 and minister of health 1960–3. Unionist MP for South Down at Westminster 1974–87.

REYNOLDS, ALBERT (b. 1932). Leader of Fianna Fail from 1992 and Taoiseach (prime minister) of the Irish Republic 1992–4.

RICHARDS, SIR BROOKS (b. 1918). Northern Ireland Security Co-ordinator 1980–2.

ROBINSON, PETER (b. 1948). Deputy Leader of the Democratic Unionist Party 1979–87 and Westminster MP for East Belfast since 1979.

TRIMBLE, DAVID (b. 1944). Westminster MP since 1990. Leader of Ulster Unionist Party since 1995.

TYRIE, ANDY (b. 1940). Commander of the Ulster Defence Association since 1973.

WEST, HARRY (b. 1917). Stormont MP 1954–72 (cabinet minister 1960–6 and 1971–2). Westminster MP February–October 1974. Leader of Ulster Unionist Party 1974–9.

Further Reading

Arthur, Paul, *The Government and Politics of Northern Ireland* (Longman, 2nd edn updated, 1987).

Aughey, Arthur, *Under Seige: Ulster Unionism and the Anglo-Irish Agreement* (Blackstaff/Hurst, 1989).

Bardon, Jonathan, *A History of Ulster* (Blackstaff, 1992).

Buckland, Patrick, *The Northern Ireland Question 1996-1986* (Historical Association, 1987).

Fanning, Ronan, *Independent Ireland* (Helicon, 1983).

Flackes, W. D., and Elliot, Sydney, *Northern Ireland: A Political Directory 1968-1993* (Blackstaff, 3rd edn, 1994).

Harkness, David, *Northern Ireland since 1920* (Helicon, 1983).

Jeffery, Keith (ed.), *The Divided Province: The Troubles in Northern Ireland 1969-85* (Orbis, 1985).

McGarry, John and O'Leary, Brendan, *Explaining Northern Ireland* (Blackwell, 1995).

Miller, David, *Queen's Rebels* (Gill and Macmillan, 1978).

Murphy, Dervla, *A Place Apart* (Penguin, 1979).

Stewart, A. T. Q., *The Narrow Ground* (Faber and Faber, 1977).

Toolis, Kevin, *Rebel Hearts* (Picador, 1995).

Whyte, John, *Interpreting Northern Ireland* (Clarendon Press, 1990).

Index

Adams, Gerry, 57, 104, 114, 135
  dialogue with John Hume, 65,
    115–17, 133
  leadership of Sinn Fein, 58, 63
  and USA, 120
Alliance party, 12, 16, 42, 51–2, 108
Amin, Idi, 98
Andrews, David, 106
Anglo-Irish Agreement, 1985
    (Hillsborough Agreement), 2,
    15, 32, 47, 117, 126, 132
  background to, 15
  international response, 82–3
  SDLP and, 61
  terms of, 17–20, 81
  unionist responses to, 14, 47,
    100–1
Anglo-Irish Joint Declaration, 1993
    (Downing Street Declaration),
    2, 24, 97, 110–19, 126
Annesley, Sir Hugh, 81, 135
army, British
  casualties, 72–3, 129
  deployment in NI, 10–11, 74–7,
    99
  withdrawal, 124, 134
  see also Royal Irish Regiment;
    Special Air Service (SAS)
    Regiment; Ulster Defence
    Regiment
Atkins, Humphrey, 14, 92

Bennett, Joseph, 77
Biaggi, Mario, 89
'Bloody Friday', 70, 131
'Bloody Sunday', 15, 69, 131
Bradford, Rev. Robert, 48, 135
Brighton, bomb at Grand Hotel, 1,
    71, 113, 132
British Commonwealth, 85, 86–7
Brooke, Peter, 101–5, 112, 135
Brookeborough, Lord, 36
Bruce, Steve, 48
Bruton, John, 134, 135
B-Specials (Ulster Special
    Constabulary), 6, 12, 55, 74,
    130

Campaign for Democracy in Ulster
    (CDU), 7
Campaign for Equal Citizenship,
    19, 125
Caradon, Lord, 86
Carey, Hugh, 90
Carrington, Lord, 92, 104
Carson, Sir Edward, 37, 45, 55,
    83–4, 135
Carter, Jimmy, 88, 91, 93
catholic(s), 3, 22, 25
  employment, 29–32
  politics, 53–65
  population in NI, 23
  social disadvantage, 26, 30–1

Channon, Paul, 57
Chichester-Clark, Major James, 9,
    44, 135
Clinton, William (Bill), 91, 93, 109,
    120, 133
Collins, Gerry, 104
Combined Loyalist Military
    Command
    cease-fire, 40, 121–2, 133
Conservative party, 125–6
Cooper, Bob, 31
Council of Ireland, 13, 84, 131
Council of Europe, 94–5
Craig, Sir James (Lord Craigavon),
    37, 55, 84, 135
Craig, William, 13, 36, 37–8, 43–4,
    135
Creasey, General Sir Timothy,
    75–6
Crossman, Richard, 99
Cuéllar, Javier Perez de, 82

Democratic Left party, 67
Democratic Unionist Party (DUP),
    18, 19
    and Joint Declaration, 119
    and Mayhew talks, 108–9
    origins and electoral fortunes,
        41–50
    policy after Anglo-Irish
        Agreement, 100, 102–3
Derry / Londonderry, 5, 99
    Bloody Sunday, 15, 69, 131
    riots, 9, 68, 130
De Lorean Motor Company, 28, 29
de Valera, Eamon, 84, 86, 135
Diplock courts, 73–4, 80
Downing Street Declaration (1969),
    11
Downing Street Declaration
    (1993), *see* Anglo-Irish Joint
    Declaration
Dungannon, 5

economy, 26–9
    British subvention to NI, 26, 99
education, 24–5
elections, 41–2
    nationalist results, 64
    unionist results, 49
Elias, Robert, 111
employment, 27–32
Enniskillen, Remembrance Sunday
    bomb, 113, 132–3
European Commission on Human
    Rights, 94–5
European Parliament, 61
European Union (formerly
    European Economic
    Community), 17, 60, 85, 94–8
    aid for NI, 96–7
    SDLP proposed role for, 107
Ewart-Biggs, Christopher, 15, 72

Fair Employment Agency (FEA),
    31–2
Fair Employment Commission
    (FEC), 31–2
Faulkner, Brian, 11, 12–13, 44, 85,
    97, 131, 135–6
Ferguson, Richard, 8
Fianna Fail party, 62, 97, 101, 108,
    116–17
Fine Gael party, 62
Fitt, Gerry (later Lord Fitt), 7,
    136
FitzGerald, Garret, 16, 97, 136
Foley, Tom, 120
Forum for Peace and
    Reconciliation, 119–20
'Framework Documents' (1995), 2,
    122, 126, 127, 134
Freeland, Lt.-Gen. Sir Ian, 11
Friends of Ireland group, 90–1
Friends of the Union, 125

Garda Siochana, 15

Gibson, Ken, 38
Gibson, Lord Justice, 72
Goodall, Sir David, 118
Goulding, Cathal, 67

Haagerup, Neils, report on NI,
    61, 95–6
Haughey, Charles J., 15–16, 132,
    136
'H-block' campaign, 16, 69
Heath, Edward (Ted), 12, 46
Hermon, Jack (Sir John), 76, 136
Hillery, Patrick, 83, 86
Hillsborough Agreement, 48
    see also Anglo-Irish Agreement
Holland, Jack, 89
housing, 5
Hume, John, 30, 62, 120, 136
    Hume–Adams dialogue, 65,
        115–17, 133
    policy after Anglo-Irish
        Agreement, 101
    and SDLP, 8, 61
    and US interest in NI, 88, 90
hunger strikes (1980–1), 16, 54–5,
    56, 131–2

Industrial Development Board
    (IDB), 28
intelligence, role in security policy,
    76–80
International Fund for Ireland,
    18, 94
internment, 12, 69, 78, 131
Ireland, *see* Republic of Ireland
Irish Independence Party, 59
Irish National Caucus, 29, 89–90
Irish National Liberation Army
    (INLA), 67–8, 78
    see also Irish Republican Socialist
        Party
Irish Northern Aid Committee, *see*
    Noraid

Irish Republican Army (IRA), 10,
    22, 35, 48, 54
    see also Official IRA; Provisional
        IRA
Irish Republican Socialist Party, 67
    see also Irish National Liberation
        Army

Kennedy, Senator Edward (Ted),
    90, 91
King, Tom, 100

Labour party (Ireland), 62, 116–17
La Mon House restaurant, 71
Lawson, Gen. Sir Richard, 76
Local Enterprise Development Unit
    (LEDU), 28
Londonderry, *see* Derry /
    Londonderry
Lynch, Jack, 83, 97, 136

MacBride, Sean, 29, 136
MacBride Principles, 29–30, 31, 93
McCartney, Robert, 19, 122, 125
McCusker, Harold, 136–7
McGuinness, Martin, 57, 102,
    114, 136
McManus, Father Sean, 89–90
MacStiofain, Sean, 57, 70, 136
Major, John, 119, 120, 133
Makarios, Archbishop, 98
Mason, Roy, 14
Maudling, Reginald, 36
Mayhew, Sir Patrick, 105, 106–10,
    136
MI5, 79
Miller, David, 55
Milosz, Czeslaw, 123
Molyneaux, James (Jim), 18, 50–1,
    92, 107, 137
Morrison, Danny, 59, 137
Mountbatten, Lord, 15, 72, 76,
    131

Moynihan, Senator Patrick, 90
Murphy, Dervla, 21

Nationalist party, 8, 59–60
Neave, Airey, 46, 131
Nelson, Brian, 77–8, 80
New Ireland Forum, 58, 62, 63,
    132
New Ulster Political Research
    Group (NUPRG), 39, 100
Noraid (Irish Northern Aid
    Committee), 89
Northern Ireland
    population, 23–4
    religious affiliations, 23
    solutions to problems, 66, 124–8
Northern Ireland Assembly, 16, 18,
    37, 41, 62
Northern Ireland Civil Rights
    Association (NICRA), 5
Northern Ireland Constitutional
    Convention, 14, 39, 43, 47
Northern Ireland Labour Party
    (NILP), 51
Northern Ireland parliament
    (Stormont), 7, 8, 11–12, 34

Official IRA, 56, 67, 78
    see also Irish Republican Army;
    Workers' Party
O'Kennedy, Michael, 98
Oldfield, Sir Maurice, 76, 137
O'Neill, Captain Terence, 6–9, 25,
    36, 37, 46, 130, 137
O'Neill, 'Tip', 90, 91–2
Orange Order, 7, 46
Orange Volunteers, 13

Paisley, Rev. Ian, 6–7, 8, 13, 36, 38,
    126, 137
    fundamentalist politics, 41
    leadership of DUP, 42, 43–4,
        47–8, 50

opposition to Anglo-Irish
    process, 83–4
'Peace People', 131
Peck, Sir John, 86–7, 88
People's Democracy (PD), 6
Pinochet, Augusto, President,
    98
police, *see* Royal Ulster
    Constabulary
Pope Paul VI, 98
Powell, Enoch, 19, 46, 48, 137
    conspiracy theories about NI, 85,
        92, 95
    and EU, 95, 96
powersharing
    consistent British policy, 126
    executive, 12–13, 14, 60
Prior, James, 47, 62
Progressive Democrats party, 108
Progressive Unionist Party (PUP),
    40
protestant(s), 3, 6, 22, 26, 125
    employment, 29
    politics, 34–52, 112
    population in NI, 23
    reaction to Anglo-Irish
        Agreement, 32, 37, 39
    reaction to Framework
        Documents, 32
Protestant Unionist Party, 41
    see also Democratic Unionist
        Party
Provisional IRA, 66, 67, 101, 119
    cease-fire, 119, 120–1, 122,
        133
    origins and early development,
        56–8
    relations with Sinn Fein, 113–14
    and republican tradition, 54–5
    security operations against, 76–80
    strategy and tactics, 68–73, 76,
        113
    US support for, 88–90, 93

see also Irish Republican Army;
Sinn Fein
Provisional Sinn Fein, *see* Sinn
Fein

Reagan, Ronald, 17, 91, 93
Rees, Merlyn, 13
religion, 22–4
see also catholic(s); protestant(s)
Republic of Ireland
1916 declaration of, 54, 55, 56
1937 constitution, 35, 130
attitudes to NI, 32, 85–6
Fianna Fail / Labour coalition,
116–17
and Joint Declaration, 118
and Mayhew talks, 108
policy after Anglo-Irish
Agreement, 101, 103–4
relations with United Kingdom,
86–8, 95–7
role in NI affairs, 13, 14–17,
83
terrorism in, 14–15
Republican Sinn Fein, 58, 113
Reynolds, Albert, 120, 137
Richards, Sir Brooks, 76, 137
Robinson, Peter, 137
Rose, Richard, 65
Royal Irish Rangers, 12
Royal Irish Regiment (RIR), 12,
74–5, 81, 125, 133
casualties, 72–3
size, 74
see also Ulster Defence Regiment
Royal Ulster Constabulary (RUC),
6, 9, 19, 124
casualties, 72, 129
reform of, 12, 127
role in security policy, 10–11, 75,
77, 78–9, 81
size, 74
Stalker report, 78–9

security policy, 73–81
implementation, 56–7
transferred to London, 12, 131
security statistics, 129
Sinn Fein, 55, 58, 59, 102, 109, 110
abandons abstentionism in
Republic, 112–13
competition with SDLP, 61–5
dialogue with SDLP, 115–17
and Forum for Peace and
Reconciliation, 120
and Joint Declaration, 119
policy after Anglo-Irish
Agreement, 113–14
see also Republican Sinn Fein
Social Democratic and Labour
Party (SDLP), 8, 12, 14, 44,
102, 112
boycotts Assembly, 16
competition with Sinn Fein,
61–5
dialogue with Sinn Fein, 115–17
electoral fortunes, 63–4
formation, 59–60, 130
and Mayhew talks, 107–8
policies and development, 60–5
policy after Anglo-Irish
Agreement, 101, 103–5
social policy, 25–6
Special Air Service (SAS)
Regiment, 76–7
Spring, Dick, 117
Stalker, John, 78–9
Stephen, Sir Ninian, 105
Stevens, John, 80
Stormont, *see* Northern Ireland
parliament
Sunningdale agreement, 47, 131
'supergrass' system, 77–8, 80, 132

Thatcher, Margaret, 15–16, 20, 46,
71, 91, 93, 133
'Third Force', 37, 48, 58, 83

Tighe, Michael, 78
Trimble, David, 137
Tyrie, Andy, 38, 137

Ulster Clubs movement, 37, 58
Ulster Covenant (1912), 55
Ulster Defence Association (UDA),
    13, 37–8, 39, 40, 48, 77–8, 80
see also New Ulster
    Political Research Group
Ulster Defence Regiment, 12,
    80, 130
casualties, 72–3, 129
character of, 74–5
size, 74, 75
see also Royal Irish Regiment
Ulster Democratic Party (UDP), 40
Ulster Loyalist Central
    Co-ordinating Committee, 37
Ulster Political Research Group
    (UPRG), 39
Ulster Resistance, 37, 48, 100
Ulster Special Constabulary
    Association, 13
Ulster Unionist Party (UUP), 5, 7,
    8, 34–52
and Anglo-Irish Agreement, 17,
    18–20
electoral fortunes and
    competition with DUP,
    41–50
and Joint Declaration, 119
and Mayhew talks, 108–9
policy after Anglo-Irish
    Agreement, 100–1, 102–3

Ulster Volunteer Force (UVF)
pre-1914 organization, 55, 130
since 1966, 13, 37–8
Ulster Workers' Council (UWC)
strike, 13–14, 37, 58, 131
unemployment, 27
United Kingdom
relations with Republic of
    Ireland, 82–3, 86–8, 95–7
subvention to NI, 26, 99
United Nations, 17, 82, 83, 87
United States of America (USA),
    17, 85, 86
aid for NI, 94
attitudes to NI problem,
    88–94
investment in NI, 29–30
United Ulster Unionist Council
    (UUUC), 13, 39, 48
Utley, T. E., 99

Vance, Cyrus, 92
Vanguard Unionist Party (VUP),
    37, 39, 42, 43

Warrington bombs, 72, 133
West, Harry, 19, 43, 44, 137
Whitelaw, William, 12, 57
Wilson, Harold, 7, 13, 76
Workers' Party, 67
see also Official IRA

Young, Sir Arthur, 11, 12

Printed in the United States
98554LV00005B/40-42/A